Discovering Feminist Philosophy

feminist constructions

Series Editors: Hilde Lindemann Nelson,
Sara Ruddick, and Margaret Urban Walker

Feminist Constructions publishes accessible books that send feminist ethics in promising new directions. Feminist ethics has excelled at critique, identifying masculinist bias in social practice and in the moral theory that is used to justify that practice. The series continues the work of critique, but its emphasis falls on construction. Moving beyond critique, the series aims to build a positive body of theory that extends feminist moral understandings.

Forthcoming books in the series by

Amy R. Baehr, Joan Mason-Grant, Diana Tietjens Meyers, Ruth Groenhout

Discovering Feminist Philosophy

Knowledge, Ethics, Politics

Robin May Schott

ROWMAN & LITTLEFIELD PUBLISHERS, INC.
Lanham • Boulder • New York • Oxford

ROWMAN & LITTLEFIELD PUBLISHERS, INC.

Published in the United States of America
by Rowman & Littlefield Publishers, Inc.
A wholly owned subsidiary of the Rowman & Littlefield Publishing Group, Inc.
4501 Forbes Boulevard, Suite 200, Lanham, Maryland 20706
www.rowmanlittlefield.com

PO Box 317
Oxford
OX2 9RU, UK

British Library Cataloguing in Publication Information Available

Library of Congress Cataloging-in-Publication Data

Schott, Robin May.
  Discovering feminist philosophy : knowledge, ethics, politics / Robin May Schott.
    p. cm.—(Feminist constructions)
  Includes bibliographical references and index.
  ISBN 0-7425-1454-4 (hardcover : alk. paper)—ISBN 0-7425-1455-2 (pbk. : alk. paper)
  1. Feminist theory. I. Title. II. Series.

  HQ1206 .S4415 2003
  305.42'01—dc21

                                                                              2003001592

Printed in the United States of America

♾™ The paper used in this publication meets the minimum requirements of
American National Standard for Information Sciences—Permanence of
Paper for Printed Library Materials, ANSI/NISO Z39.48-1992.

"Robin May Schott shows us the ways in which feminist interventions in interpreting the philosophical tradition and feminist analyses of oppression, subjectivity, and recognition are central to the philosophical tasks of our times."

—Debra Bergoffen, George Mason University

"This book offers much more than an engaging, accessible introduction into the main debates in feminist philosophy. It shows that a critical encounter between philosophy and feminism is vital not only for the reflection on the politics of knowledge but also for the future of philosophy."

—Ewa Ziarek, University of Notre Dame

"This book challenges irrational, hostile, and even 'hysterical' reactions to feminist philosophy from those in the mainstream of the profession. From her perspective as a migrant philosopher, Schott demonstrates the importance of feminist theorizing to a range of philosophical and broad intellectual debates. Schott's outsider's critique of academic philosophy should be read by outsiders and insiders, feminists and anti-feminists, and all students of philosophy who think the field should concern itself with the most urgent and difficult questions facing societies today."

—Laurie Shrage, California State
Polytechnic University

In loving memory of Eric Allen Hill (1952–1994), whose vision as a black philosopher nurtured and deepened my vision of feminist philosophy.

Contents

~

Acknowledgments

I would like to thank Finn Collin, for his belief in philosophical pluralism and his proposal that I take on this project. Bente Rosenbeck, original copartner in this project, has subsequently acted as a valued critic. I am grateful to Hilde Nelson and Sara Ruddick, series coeditors for Rowman and Littlefield, for their enthusiasm for the English publication of this book. Sara Ruddick has been a tireless and acute reader, providing careful and invaluable suggestions. And I would like to thank Niels Thomassen, who shows the broadness of philosophical spirit that institutions of philosophy need to flourish. I am very grateful to Claudia Card and Libby Tata Arcel for providing vital suggestions for research materials related to war rape. I am deeply indebted to Svetlana Slapsak and Mirsad Tokaca for generously giving me their publications when we met at a conference, cosponsored by the Danish Center for Holocaust and Genocide Studies, in Copenhagen in spring 2002. I am also grateful to the Institut für die Wissenschaften vom Menschen (IWM) in Vienna, where I was provided with office facilities and peace of mind to make the final revisions on this book. And I would like to thank David Soucek of the IWM for saving me hours of work and aggravation in the final disk preparation.

INTRODUCTION

~

Why This Book?

Who will read this book? What imaginary reader do I take as my conversational partner? On the one hand, since I am a professional philosopher, my audience would seem to target professional philosophers. Yet many professional philosophers are characterized by something other than indifference to feminist philosophy. I have witnessed several instances where academic philosophers erupt in outright hostility at the mere mention of the term. I cannot think of any other area of philosophy that produces such outbursts of passionate contempt by individuals who pride themselves on the professionalism of their reason. In this climate, I am aware that I will be taking up a discourse that might be read by an unwilling audience. Nonetheless, I hope that this book will provide resources for moving away from entrenched prejudices that are based on ignorance and some half-forgotten memory of what feminist activism was like twenty-five years ago.

On the other hand, the book might be better directed toward a willing audience—readers who are not professional philosophers, but who do have an interest in feminism. Such readers are less interested in the question, "How can feminist philosophy be made palatable to those with different philosophical dispositions?" than they are in the question, "What intellectual resources are offered by feminist philosophy?" Facing this dilemma of what audience to target was one of my major challenges while writing this book.

Despite these difficulties, I undertook the project of writing this book in the spirit of affirming the insights made possible by my immigrant identity. Having lived in Denmark for more than ten years is not enough to make me Danish—a fact made apparent to others by the first sentence out of my mouth. For me it is confirmed daily through my children—hearing the songs they learn that were not part of my childhood and helping them with their Danish homework, which requires continual checks with the dictionary. Nor am I simply American anymore. The life I would have lived in the United States has also become foreign to me. My composite identity has obvious disadvantages (linguistic, professional, familial, bureaucratic), but it has some advantages as well. This composite identity has given me some insights into the paradoxes of Danish culture and has situated me as a witness to the cross-cultural encounter that takes place in the meeting between Danish philosophers and non-Danish feminist philosophers.

Over the years I have had occasion to invite several American women philosophers to Denmark. They are all stunned by the gap between the strong representation of women in the Danish government and the weak representation of women in the academy.[1] The numbers of female ministers in Denmark (27.8 percent after the 2001 election) far exceeds what one could dream of in the American government; the numbers of women represented in parliament (36.9 percent after the 2001 election) are likewise impressive compared with the numbers of women in Congress (after the 2000 election, 13 percent in the Senate and 13.8 percent in the House of Representatives). The Danish welfare state is comparatively women- (or family-) friendly in the area of maternity leave. The six-month paid maternity leave previously allotted to women has increased to twelve months.[2] By contrast, in the United States, the 1993 Family and Medical Leave Act permits workers to take up to twelve weeks *unpaid* leave for a variety of medical conditions, including childbirth. More attractive benefits are available only to women who work for companies that voluntarily offer some paid maternity leave. The International Labor Organization, a United Nations agency, called the maternity leave benefits in the United States the least generous in the industrial world.[3] Despite the comparatively progressive situation in Denmark, the number of women teaching in permanent positions in Danish universities has not changed significantly over the last twenty years. Although for many years women have made up the majority of the student population (currently 58 percent of new students at the University of Copenhagen are women), women account for only 19 percent of assistant and associate professors and only 8 percent of professors.[4] The University of Copenhagen refused to implement a proposal for increasing the number of women faculty put forth in 1998 by a committee that the former rector himself had established.

In other areas of social life as well, there is a marked ambivalence toward women's situation. Although Danes have a deep-rooted sense of their freedom (hence the permissiveness regarding pornography, which propelled Denmark into the international limelight in the 1960s), the government has been reluctant to address the real limitations on freedom experienced by women who are victims of domestic violence. In 1999, the Ministries of Education, Justice, and Health all refused to fund an initiative by the "Social Udviklingscenter" to begin educational programs about violence against women. Violence is presumably best seen as a problem of foreigners—in the Balkans or among immigrants to Denmark —and not as a problem within Danish domestic life. And although the Little Mermaid has been repeatedly decapitated, no one to my knowledge has deconstructed this national symbol from the point of view of gender. Perhaps it is more comfortable to believe Disney's ending than to address the tragic fate of the mermaid in H. C. Andersen's tale, within a secular world view.

When I chose for family reasons to resign my permanent position at the University of Louisville and move to Denmark, my choice was enabled by my positive predisposition to Danish culture. Danes had treated the Jews better than most other peoples in Europe during World War II, even if the Danish record is not unblemished. The Danish welfare net is light-years ahead of that found in the United States and helps children have a decent quality of life in this country. Danes also value the rituals of social life by which they seek out the company of family and friends. Since I expected to find in Danish culture a respect for difference and an interest in strengthening social bonds, it was with shock and incredulity that I, as a feminist philosopher, was confronted by hostility and disparagement instead. I want to emphasize that I also have met with sympathy and positive support from a few colleagues and from many students. But the negativity belied my expectations of Danish culture and has marked this cultural encounter. Of course, these difficulties were exacerbated by the bleak situation for women philosophers in Denmark more generally. When I was appointed visiting associate professor in the University of Copenhagen's Philosophy Department in 1995, I was the first woman ever to hold a full-time position in the department. In 2003, there are still no women who have permanent positions in this department.

Not that being a woman philosopher or a feminist philosopher in the United States is an easy business either. When I walked into the philosophy department at Yale University for the first time in 1977, at the beginning of my graduate studies, the departmental secretary said, "Hello, Robin." When I asked with surprise how she knew my name, she answered, "The other one was already in here." Graduate studies in philosophy was indeed a male-dominated discipline. I remember being the only woman in a Kant seminar with twenty men who smelled like they had just walked out of the men's locker room. I was glad to be able to lay *my* pocket watch on the table—a gift from my parents on my return from studying philosophy in Germany—across from my professor and *his* pocket watch. Discovering feminist philosophy helped me deal with my outsider status. It first occurred to me that I was an outsider when one of my professors from Swarthmore College asked me at my graduation reception: "Tell me, Robin, why have there been no great women philosophers?" Though I had passed my exams with high honors, this question seemed to delegitimate my choice of a career in philosophy. Later, in graduate school, discovering work by feminist philosophers helped me answer the question about the "missing women"[5] in philosophy. Feminist philosophy helped prevent me from becoming a missing woman in philosophy, by showing that an outsider status can generate key philosophical questions.

While I was at Yale in the late 1970s, the National Endowment for the Humanities granted money to several women faculty to run a two-year interdisciplinary seminar in women's studies, which became a centerpiece in educating graduate students and faculty in this new field. It was the struggles of feminist graduate and undergraduate students and women faculty in the 1970s and 1980s that put feminist phi-

losophy on the agenda in U.S. academic departments. When I joined
the philosophy department at the University of Louisville in 1983, not
all faculty members were sympathetic to the field. (One, an ex-priest,
asked me where I was hiding my whip when he saw me wear a black
leather skirt to work.) Nonetheless, feminist philosophy has gained
enough institutional recognition that scholarship has flourished in
this field.

Perhaps the negativity toward feminist philosophy that I have
met in Denmark should not have surprised me, since very few
women have had full-time positions in philosophy in this country.
So women have not had the opportunity to provide competent
teaching and publishing in feminist philosophy—and men certainly
have not done it either. The hostility toward the field is also rooted
partly in prejudices that I only lately have had pointed out to me.
Many people in this milieu (both students and professionals) apparently believe that feminist philosophers assert that women's reason
is different from men's, and therefore that women and men cannot
communicate. Some students draw what they believe is the logical
conclusion: they should not try to understand what feminists say,
since feminists have defined their point of view as noncommunica-
ble. I can only speculate about the origin of these beliefs, since they
have nothing to do with the work of feminist philosophers over the
last quarter of a century. Could there have been student activists in
the 1980s whose interests were caught by one thread of the debate,
e.g., about gender differences in thinking or in morality?[6] Given the
lack of professional context for working through feminist ideas, did
women students develop a rhetoric that alienated men? But even if
this scenario were true, how have these prejudices been reproduced
in subsequent generations of students? The reproduction of prejudice and ignorance is circular: the absence of a professional context
for feminist philosophy produces ignorance and prejudice about it,
which ensures that there will be no professional context for this
field. And a will to ignorance about feminist philosophy is produced
by certain philosophical convictions about the nature of truth, universality, and reality that dominate philosophical debates. Those
inside the milieu of philosophy claim that feminist philosophy reduces philosophy to politics or sociology, and thus it undermines

the essential features of philosophy. In the remainder of this introduction, I will focus on the presuppositions I have met that complicate the intellectual encounter between feminism and philosophy.

In preparing this introduction, I read over notes I wrote after speaking on feminist epistemologies in a seminar on the foundations of knowledge sponsored by philosophy students at the University of Copenhagen in March 1998. The seminar was an unusually unpleasant experience for me. I had on several occasions offered courses related to feminist philosophy in the Philosophy Department, and students who chose these courses were enthusiastic. But this was an occasion where a large group of students, mostly men, were "forced" to read one article by a feminist theorist. (All four of the presenters at the seminar were asked to provide one article in advance as suggested reading.) The comments that followed my talk were markedly hostile. But in retrospect they were also fruitful, since they pointed to a number of prejudices and misunderstandings about feminist philosophy that I seek to debunk. And in revealing mistaken assumptions about feminist philosophy, the comments also revealed some common presuppositions about what "real philosophy" is taken to be. In what follows, I respond to the objections posed to me during the seminar.

1 *Objection: Feminism posits a natural dualism between the sexes and therefore is not relevant to women today.*

This objection posits an identification between feminism and the claim for sexual dualism. However, sexual dualism is not plausible, since the social changes of the last thirty years have proved that women can do everything that men can do. But feminism demands that women mark themselves out *as women*, even though sexual equality now exists. And women no longer want to mark themselves *as women*. (As one woman put it, she wanted to be characterized by what was between her ears, not between her legs.) Hence, the objection states that feminism is not relevant to women today.

Reply: To reply to the first part of the objection, one must first ask whether feminism does posit a natural dualism between the sexes. The question of sexual difference is a central issue in contemporary feminist discussions, and there are a range of views on this issue. On one end of the spectrum, the French philosopher Luce Irigaray has argued for the omnipresence of sexual dualism in Western culture. In the opening to

An Ethics of Sexual Difference, she writes: "Sexual difference is one of the major philosophical issues, if not the issue, of our age. . . . Sexual difference is probably the issue in our time which could be our 'salvation' if we thought it through."[7] Irigaray is one of the feminist philosophers who seek to affirm the existence of sexual dualism as an avenue for genuine recognition and ethical love between the sexes. On the other end of the spectrum, Judith Butler seeks to problematize sexual difference as itself an effect of norms. She is interested in exploring "how normative criteria form the matter of bodies."[8] For Butler, the task is to analyze the process of materialization by which sexed bodies come to be and to refute any arguments for a natural sexual dualism. Her views have had enormous popular appeal, because she seems to show the possibility of subverting the normative process by which bodies become heterosexual male or female bodies. Thus, she articulates a space for ambiguously sexed bodies with desires that subvert these norms.

Therefore, although feminist philosophers do problematize sexual difference, there is no agreement about the constitution of sexual difference, the merits of its affirmation, or the possibility of its subversion.

To reply to the second part of the objection, why should women bother with feminism today? Although most feminists distance themselves from an essentialist view of sexual difference, they do point to the contemporary need for feminist theory and politics. Women may have proven that they can do everything that men can do, but does that make gender identity irrelevant? Life experiences show that Simone de Beauvoir was right in claiming that a woman is one who is in the situation of being a woman. The situation of being a woman includes seeing widespread pornography and advertisements that eroticize the female body to sell consumer goods. For many, being a woman also implies difficult choices regarding children and work.[9]

Recognizing that gender identity shapes people's lives does not mean that women's reason is different from men's reason. But it might mean that women are interested in raising different kinds of questions to philosophy than men typically have raised. For example, feminist philosophers draw from a number of different theoretical fields—including phenomenology, psychoanalysis, and deconstruction—to contribute sophisticated analyses of bodies and of materiality. Since phenomenologists like Maurice Merleau-Ponty have analyzed the bodily roots of awareness, why should the sexed/gendered aspects of human bodies be excluded from philosophical view?[10] By including analyses of sex and gender in contemporary discussions of the human body, identity, and knowledge, feminists challenge the ways in which certain questions have dominated philosophical debates and other questions have been marginalized or excluded from philosophical view. For example, the Canadian philosopher Lorraine Code, in her article "Taking Subjectivities into Account," criticizes the assumption in mainstream epistemology that propositions in the form S-knows-that-p capture the essence of knowledge. This assumption excludes consideration of the role of subjectivity in epistemology: e.g., how subjectivities produce epistemologies, and how knowing other people (instead of observing objects) can be taken as an exemplary kind of knowing.[11]

Feminists give critical attention to the process by which certain kinds of philosophical questions become legitimated and other kinds are refused legitimation. They ask, What is the relation between dominant and marginalized discourses? What is the nature of knowledge/power relations? What strategies are available for decentering dominant discourses? Hence, they often draw inspiration from theoretical work that analyzes questions of legitimation, authorization, power, and subversion, including texts by marxist and postmarxist authors, Michel Foucault, and Jacques Derrida.

Hence, feminist theory is relevant both to contemporary women—and to philosophical debates that reach far beyond explicit discussions of gender and sex.

Objection: Feminist philosophy is of interest only to women, not to men.

This objection builds on the first, that of a dualism between the sexes. Feminism is not only based on sexual dualism, but it addresses only the female pole of this dualism. Hence, it has no relevance to men.

Reply: In 1869, John Stuart Mill wrote in the Subjection of Women, "Women cannot be expected to devote themselves to the emancipation of women, until men in considerable number are prepared to join with them in the undertaking."[12] Mill argued for men's obligation to support women's emancipation in order to further the development of humanity. Women's emancipation would enhance their role as moral educators of children, provide conditions for a greater union of thoughts and inclinations in married life, and double the mental faculties available for serving humanity.[13]

In 1949, Simone de Beauvoir shifted the focus from the benefits accrued to humanity by the emancipation of women to a critical interrogation of the concept of humanity itself. In *The Second Sex* she explicitly linked notions of humanity and rationality to norms of masculinity.

> It amounts to this: just as for the ancients there was an absolute vertical with reference to which the oblique was defined, so there is an absolute human type, the masculine. Woman has ovaries, a uterus; these peculiarities imprison her in her subjectivity, circumscribe her within the limits of her own nature. It is often said that she thinks with her glands. Man superbly ignores the fact that his anatomy also includes glands, such as the testicles, and that they secrete hormones. He thinks of his body as a direct and normal connection with the world, which he believes he apprehends objectively, whereas he regards the body of woman as a hindrance, a prison, weighed down by everything peculiar to it. . . . Thus humanity is male and man defines woman not in herself but as relative to him. . . . He is the Subject, he is the Absolute—she is the Other.[14]

This key passage in Beauvoir's text initiated a thoroughgoing analysis by later feminists of the ways in which the terms "humanity," "masculinity," and "femininity" are defined in relation to each other. For example, the Australian philosopher Elizabeth Grosz argues that the task of feminist philosophy is "to be able to recognize how the world is coded according to masculine or feminine attributes and associations, how knowledges, theories, discourses, function by excluding, expelling, or neglecting the contributions of femininity and women, producing lacks, gaps, absences about femininity which are necessary for these theories to operate; and how these theories distribute value according to the privileging of one sex over the other." And she goes on to define the phallocentrism that underlies much of the Western philosophical tradition as occurring "whenever the two sexes are represented by a singular—or 'human' (i.e., masculine)—model."[15] In her book *Yielding Gender*, the

Australian philosopher Penelope Deutscher further analyzes how contradictory representations of women have the effect of sustaining the philosophical identification of maleness with rationality.[16]

Therefore, the concepts of humanity and rationality in the Western philosophical tradition have been embroiled in contradictory definitions of and alliances between masculinity and femininity. As such, feminist philosophy is relevant to all those working with the history of philosophy and its inherited presuppositions.

③ *Objection: Feminist philosophy reduces philosophy to politics or sociology, etc., hence, it cannot be a legitimate philosophical project.*

This objection argues that feminism is guilty of one or many forms of reductionism: feminism reduces philosophy to politics, to sociology, to anthropology, or to psychology. Since feminism takes as its starting point questions about men or women, it belongs in the realm of empirical studies and not in the realm of philosophy.

Reply: This objection presupposes a sharp distinction between empirical and theoretical sciences. It considers philosophy to be a meta-reflection that may provide the foundation for empirical sciences but that must be sharply distinguished from these other disciplines. It argues that rationality is not reducible to the social context or interests that may affect scientific development. This position acknowledges that one may uncover interests or errors in the scientific enterprise. But the rational dimension of science remains untouched by these specific empirical factors. In other words, this objection presupposes a hard border that separates inquiries into truth and inquiries into power. Although this view of the protected status of rationality is certainly a powerful strain within Western philosophy, it is hardly the only philosophical conception of reason that has been influential. A wide range of prominent philosophers, such as G. W. H. Hegel, Karl Marx, Søren Kierkegaard, Friedrich Nietzsche, and Merleau-Ponty, focus on aspects of rationality that reveal it to be less than fully independent of context and historical development. They argue that reasoning is itself a temporal process that is embodied in subjective and social struggles. One does not destroy reason or science by pointing to the complex dynamics of what Foucault calls the power/knowledge tension. One destroys only the myth that there is an essential core of reason or science that is fully self-sufficient.

Many, though certainly not all, feminist philosophers are sympathetic to the enlarged conception of rationality inspired by these philosophers in the Continental tradition. Their project is not to destroy rationality, but to revise conceptions of reason in relation to context, embodiment, subjectivity, and social identity. Exploring the philosophical significance of the existence of both men and women (instead of focusing on "human beings") is not a reduction of philosophy to nonphilosophical concerns. Rather, it is an argument for a conception of philosophy that is self-reflective about its history, conversational partners, and effects. It does not close down but opens up avenues for philosophical inquiry. It poses the following kinds of questions: What is the subject of philosophy? Is this subject humanity? Does humanity have a universal nature? Does universality implicitly carry with it certain exclusions? Does the sexual differentiation of human beings have implications for philosophical inquiry? Feminist philosophers problematize the term "humanity" in relation to all areas of philosophy—e.g., aesthetics, epistemology, ethics, history of philosophy, metaphysics, philosophy of language, and political philosophy.

Thus, feminism does not reduce philosophy to politics. But it does criticize the reduced version of the type of academic philosophy that seeks to legitimize itself by imposing hard borders to separate "real philosophy" from other fields of inquiry. Feminist philosophy, instead, can be viewed as a project that is loyal to the originary conception of philosophy as a quest to deepen self-reflection in all human inquiries.

Objection: Feminists' focus on sexual difference undermines the concept of universality and thus undermines the possibility of philosophy.

This objection argues that because feminists pose questions relating to the existence of men and women, they cannot develop universal concepts about humanity. Such universals, it is argued, are necessary for philosophy in general and moral philosophy in particular. Furthermore, this objection condemns feminists by the following argument: If one difference (like sexual difference) is allowed to be philosophically legitimate, then any difference (like hair color) must also be philosophically significant. But if any difference is philosophically significant, then philosophy is concerned with trivial, accidental features of human existence and no longer focuses on what is essential to humanity. Since philosophy is not concerned with trivial, accidental features of human existence, then differences (e.g., sexual difference) cannot be philosophically significant. Hence, feminism's attempt to analyze difference ends in trivialization and undermines its own stated goals.

Reply: To reply to the first part of the objection about the status of universals in philosophy: The concept of universality has been debated throughout the history of philosophy, and it remains contentious today. On the one hand, philosophers inspired by Immanuel Kant, for example, argue that universal rational concepts are necessary to have knowledge or morality at all. On the other hand, philosophers inspired by Marx or Nietzsche or their twentieth-century heirs point out that abstract concepts like universality are themselves historically mutable. The shift in the position and function of universality within a philosophical system gives an indication of broader historical changes.[17] These theorists point to contradictions that are immanent in theories about universality. For example, although Kant claimed that all human beings are rational ends-in-themselves, he excluded women, Jews, and servants from possessing full rational agency. Thus, the concept of universality is itself no guarantee that all human beings will be included within its normative reach, and the argument for the practical necessity of universal norms is weakened.

Feminist philosophers can be found on both sides of the debate about universality. For example, Martha Nussbaum, who has become engaged with problems of international development, has developed an analysis of human capabilities that is based on a "universalist account of central human functions, closely allied to a form of political liberalism." Nussbaum argues that only a universalist account of human functions—e.g., of bodily health and integrity—can provide an adequate account of each and every person's capabilities and a basis of constitutional principles that should be implemented by the governments of all nations.[18] Seyla Benhabib, who critically develops Habermas's philosophy, also seeks to defend the tradition of universalism. She argues that one can develop a defense of universalism without the metaphysical props that so many feminists have criticized. She argues for a universalism that is "interactive, not legislative, cognizant of gender difference not gender blind, contextually sensitive and not situation indifferent."[19]

Feminists inspired by French poststructuralism, on the other hand, are generally skeptical about claims for universality. They point out that universality always brings about certain exclusions, e.g., the exclusion of women from the category of humanity, the exclusion of lesbian women from the category of women, and the exclusion of women of color from the category of feminist. Universality may have strategic significance in debates about human rights. But the history of human rights declarations seems to prove either the weak claim, that universals are inadequate in their reach, or the strong claim, that the structure of universality is exclusionary. The United Nations deemed it necessary to draw up subsequent declarations and conventions for the rights of the child and to protect women against discrimination and violence, as a supplement to the *Universal Declaration of Human Rights* adopted in 1948. Thus, feminists are interested in moral and political projects of emancipation and resistance, but there is no consensus among feminists about the contribution of universality to these projects.

To the second part of the objection dealing with the status of difference: This objection asserts that any specificities that qualify the subject humanity lead down the slippery slope of trivialization: if one analyzes the significance of sex, why not analyze eye color or hairstyle? But feminists do not assert that any difference will do as an object of inquiry; they are interested in differences that count—which include a wide range of differences, such as gender, sexual preference, race, class, ethnicity, nationality, and religion. These differences count not because they lay a natural claim to our attention but because the social world makes them count. If the social world made eye color decisive for an individual's opportunities to thrive (as in the famous case of the elementary school teacher who taught her students a lesson about racism by showing preferences on succeeding days to students with blue or brown eyes), then that would be a significant difference. And despite their disclaimers, philosophers have generally treated sexual difference as a difference that counts.[20] Thus, feminists have shown that it is productive, not self-defeating, to analyze philosophically concrete differences of identities.

Objection: Feminists are explicitly interested in how features of existence (e.g., gender) or knowledge are socially and historically constructed. Thus, either (a) they are indifferent to the fundamental questions of philosophy about the underlying nature of the world and of truth, or (b) they reject the

view that there is such an underlying nature. If feminists argue for the first position, then they demonstrate their inability to grasp the truly philosophical questions. If feminists argue for the second position, then they have aligned themselves with a poor philosophical position—namely, relativism. Thus, feminists either are not philosophers at all or they are poor philosophers.

Reply: This objection is structured by the metaphor of surface vs. depth. It claims that since feminists are interested in questions of construction, then by implication they overlook questions about what is underneath that which is constructed. This position is viewed as tantamount to denying that there are any facts at all. As one student said to me, surely feminists want some facts that are rock solid, like that the Holocaust really occurred.

Feminists in the 1980s would have responded to this objection as follows: It is true that feminist research focuses on the difference between what is constructed (e.g., gender) and what lies underneath this construction (e.g., the biological, sexed body). But it is mistaken to claim that social construction is mere surface, whereas reality is found underneath this surface. What is decisive for human beings is how they live their bodies in the world, since one can never experience presocial bodies. Extending this position to other areas of intellectual research does not deny historical facts. Rather, social constructionism helps one examine how historical phenomena such as the Holocaust are socially created, rather than viewing such phenomena as natural or inevitable.

Feminists in the 1990s, having drawn inspiration from French poststructuralist debates, would have replied to this objection somewhat differently: The metaphor of surface–depth, which implies that there is a subject that shapes a pre-given object, is simply wrong. Instead, as in the account offered by Judith Butler in *Bodies that Matter*, construction of reality is a process by which both subjects and their acts become visible.[21] Butler argues that "there is no reference to a pure body which is not at the same time a further formation of that body."[22] Hence, interrogations about "reality" must be themselves critically interrogated for the manner in which they produce the phenomenon that they propose to examine. This reformulation of the notion of construction has, according to Butler, the following implications about sex: "The category of 'sex' is, from the start, normative; it is what Foucault has called a 'regulatory ideal.'"[23] Butler's analysis is not only a theory of sex, but also a theory about the nature of materiality. As such, it is a significant contribution to an understanding of the relation between norms, actions, and historical reality and not a dismissal of these concerns.

Feminist philosophers also have addressed explicitly metaphysical and ontological concerns, as Christine Battersby does in her book *The Phenomenal Woman*. "Philosophers have notably failed to address the ontological significance of the fact that selves are born. . . . This book . . . explores an ontology in which 'self' and 'other' intertwine in ways that allow us to think identity alongside radical novelty, power-dependencies, singularity and birth."[24] Battersby's concerns reflect the interest of many British feminist philosophers in using feminist perspectives for altering metaphysical and ontological categories. Her approach seeks to enlarge our picture of the fundamental nature of reality, and she explicitly distances herself from debates about constructionism that have been so important for feminists in the United States.

Thus, part (a) of the objection is a false description of all feminist philosophers, and part (b) is a false description of many feminists. There still remains the objection against relativism, i.e., that feminists are relativists and that relativism is not a viable philosophical position. I will defer the response to this objection to the chapter on epistemology. At this point I will just note that Linda Martín Alcoff, in her book *Real Knowing*, seeks to develop an ontology of truth that views truth as historically relative, but not as subjective or ideological.[25]

Objection: If feminist philosophers are interested in contributing to discussions that have general philosophical significance, they should not define their work as feminist. This label marginalizes their scholarship, creates an adversarial relationship with other members of the philosophical community, and detracts from the substantive philosophical contributions that they may make.

This objection argues that feminist philosophy is not *substantively* different from other kinds of philosophical investigations. Therefore, feminists should just carry out the work of philosophy. Feminist philosophers use the term "feminist" because of its *strategic*, not substantive significance. But this is a poor strategy, since it generates aggression and hostility.

Reply: People who raise this objection often have some familiarity and sympathy for feminist philosophical discussions, such as the debates about an ethic of care. These people may have read feminist texts because of their interest in other philosophical texts about love, rather than because of their interest in feminism.

Let me reply to the second part of the objection first. Is the term "feminist" used for *strategic* significance? Here I would agree with my critics that the term does have strategic significance. It points to a body of work that began with the interrogation of the significance of gender in philosophy—e.g., in history of philosophy, epistemology, ethics, aesthetics, and metaphysics. In the last two decades, feminist work has developed as an inquiry into other aspects of identity, such as race, class, ethnicity, and sexual choice, and the implications of these features for reinterpreting traditional philosophical problems. As Linda Martín Alcoff and Elizabeth Potter write, feminists both treat traditional philosophical issues in new ways and introduce new problems for philosophy, such as the politics of knowledge and the impact of the sexed body of the knower on the production of knowledge.[26]

As such, maintaining the term "feminist" has strategic significance because it enables people to track the historical development and breadth of this heterogeneous international debate. The term "feminist" is given a positive value from the vantage point of those interested in questions about gender and about the relation between perspective, context, and theory. But from the vantage point of nonsympathizers, the term "feminist" is given a negative value precisely because of its interrogation of perspective and context and because of its challenge to the view that the substantive work of philosophy is free of issues of power.

One might speculate about the time horizon in which using the label feminism will be productive. The question, "Will feminist philosophy still exist at the end of the 21st century?" was posed in the *Newsletter Women Philosophers*, published in Amsterdam in January 2000. All but one of the respondents answered in the affirmative. The exception, Veronica Vasterling, wrote that she hopes "that at the end of the 21st century 'feminist philosophy' does not exist anymore, either because there is no need anymore, or because its concerns have become part of philosophy as a whole."[27] In other words, speculating about the supersession of feminist philosophy is possible either (1) if all traces of gender hierarchies and differences in language, culture, and thought were abolished, or (2) if mainstream philosophy were transformed to incorporate feminist questions. But without these radical changes, the term "feminism" remains a positive and important strategic choice.

To return to the first part of the objection: is there a *substantive* change marked by doing feminist philosophy that is distinct from just doing philosophy? The strategic difference named by feminism also marks a difference in philosophical views. Despite the radically different ways of approaching philosophy with feminist concerns, there is one minimal commonality shared by these approaches: the thematization of sexed bodies. Although feminist philosophers draw inspiration from a wide variety of sources, they nonetheless relate these debates to questions about the existence of bodies marked by sex, and feminist philosophers have increasingly contributed to an analysis of the complex relations between sex, race, and ethnicity.

For example, Susan Neiman is a nonfeminist philosopher who makes a brilliant contribution to interpreting the role of the Unconditioned in Kant's philosophy. In her reading, the Unconditioned becomes linked to themes such as the incompleteness of knowledge, the problem of radical uncertainty, the process of knowledge, and the public and communal nature of thought.[28] As such, her work can contribute significantly to discussions of reason and knowledge taken up by feminists by posing questions such as: What motivates inquiry and assures its inevitable incompleteness? How can one view reason as realizing ethical and political goals, instead of treating these goals as extrinsic to the interests of reason? Furthermore, one can draw on Neiman's work to go beyond it by thematizing the existence of sexed and raced bodies as a question for reason, ethics, and politics. One could ask, what are the conditions that condition the existence of sexed and raced bodies and their mutual relations? How can one seek the ends that would transform actual relations between the sexes and races according to ideals of possible relations?[29] Thus, feminist work does overlap with and draw inspiration from work that is not characterized as feminist. But it relates these inquiries to feminist concerns, which are then brought to bear on philosophy generally.

⑦ *Objection: Feminists claim that their theories are better than nonfeminist theories because they have an emancipatory interest. But they cannot clarify their notion of emancipation. If feminists locate an emancipatory interest in one group, such as women, then how can they resolve the problem of conflicting emancipatory interests between groups? If feminists locate an emancipatory interest in every individual, then they are presupposing a concept of emancipation inherited from the Enlightenment that at least some feminists have criticized. And if feminists reject both of these claims, then how can they claim to be emancipatory at all?*

Reply: The first part of the objection addresses the question of collective emancipation. How can one justify that a particular group becomes privileged as a bearer of emancipatory values? How can one adjudicate conflicts between groups? When this objection was raised to me during the seminar in 1998, the example of conflicting emancipatory interests was the conflict between Israelis and Palestinians. Presumably, one could refer to the conflict between men's and women's interests in relation to affirmative action policies in the United States as well.

The notion of an emancipatory interest invested in the proletariat as a collective subject was developed by Karl Marx and later by Georg Lukács in *History and Class Consciousness*.[30] Some American feminist theorists, notably Nancy Hartsock and Sandra Harding, have adapted the notion of emancipatory interest to the "standpoint of women" in present society. I have no intention of defending such a theory—although I will return to this theme in my discussion of feminist epistemologies. However, I will note that theorists who criticize standpoint theory nonetheless maintain an emancipatory goal for theory. Alcoff and Potter write, "For feminists, the purpose of epistemology is not only to satisfy intellectual curiosity, but also to contribute to an emancipatory goal: the expansion of democracy in the production of knowledge."[31]

The issue at stake in the objection relates to the question of normativity. If competing groups are inspired by conflicting emancipatory interests, how can these claims be adjudicated? The question is structurally the same as the question about how to judge conflicts between individuals. Is the criterion for judgment transcendent—i.e., external to the group or individual relations—or is it immanent—i.e., situated within the context of these relations? This is a perennial debate in philosophy, with advocates on both sides. I myself have been most interested in exploring how normativity is immanent. In the example of conflicts between Israelis and Palestinians, one can focus on how diverse each of these groups are and how strategies for reconciliation have been generated from within each group.

The second part of the objection refers to debates amongst feminists about their relation to the Enlightenment inheritance. Some feminists argue that the Enlightenment notion of autonomy—of individual self-determination—is a precondition for the discourse of women's liberation and for the political gains that women have won. Other writers, inspired by poststructuralist theory, argue that the Enlightenment notions about the nature of reason, freedom, and the subject are antithetical to feminist politics and theory. These thinkers are committed to showing that reason is not divorced from contingent existence, that the self is embedded in social relations, that the self is embodied and thus is historically specific and partial. The second part of the objection is directed against this latter group. How can feminists argue for an emancipatory interest if they reject the view that each individual has a disembodied, rational, free will? This objection ultimately refers to the question of whether norms are context independent or context dependent. Poststructuralist theorists do not renounce the concepts of norms or emancipation as such, but they do renounce the attempt to provide transcendent justifications of these concepts.

These seven objections certainly do not constitute all of the objections that I have heard raised against feminist philosophy. But they do point to crucial misconceptions about the nature of feminist philosophy, as well as to presuppositions about philosophy's nature and scope that have made the philosophical encounter with feminism so difficult in Denmark. One must address the affective implications of this encounter as well. Professional philosophers in Denmark have been known to behave in distinctly nonprofessional ways when this theme is mentioned. And yet the students in the seminar in 1998 asked, why are feminists so aggressive? One could reasonably ask instead, why are these philosophers so aggressively opposed to this field, instead of being curious or merely indifferent? The affective response reminds one that what is at stake is not just an intellectual challenge, but a challenge to how academic power is reproduced. As Pierre Bourdieu notes in *Homo Academicus*, academic power is wielded through teachers' capacities to affect their students' expectations and objective possibilities for getting stipends and academic appointments.[32] The consequences of this power is seen in students' choices of advisor and research themes, even though many of these choices are made through what Bourdieu calls an unconscious adaptation to one's habitus. One might speculate that feminist philosophy is perceived as a potential threat to the current patterns by which academic philosophy is reproduced—a perception that is connected with the rejection of any procedure to increase the numbers of women with positions in the field.

Postindustrial societies exhibit a confusing mix of views about the situation of women and of feminism. Most people believe that women's equality has already been achieved, and all that remains are some small nuances of difference that can be easily leveled out. Yet women and men still do not receive equal wages for equal work. And poverty, discrimination, inadequate health care, and violence are a depressing reality for women around the world. To cite a few examples, five hundred thousand women die and eight million are disabled each year during pregnancy or childbirth; of these, sixty thousand are adolescent girls who die each year from complications in pregnancy or childbirth; girls compose nearly two-thirds of the 130 million children in developing countries not in school; and domestic violence continues unchallenged in many parts of the world. For example, one in five women in Hong Kong is beaten by their husbands.[33] Neither in the United States nor in an international context are the issues of feminism passé, though occasionally they may be viewed as more or less fashionable.

In such a world—in our world—it is as compelling as ever to struggle to understand the impact of the two sexes of the human species on human culture and thought. When my son Emil was nine, he announced at the dinner table his conviction that one's body and one's world view are inseparably linked: his body was made like Daddy's and his sister Maya's body was like Mommy's. So he could understand

Daddy better and Maya could understand Mommy better. And wouldn't he look funny with underpants that had flowers on them? I might not share all of my son's convictions, but after having listed the arguments of academic philosophers who deny any connection between (1) the existence of men *and* women and (2) the shape of philosophical theories, it is refreshing to have a child once again notice when the emperor is wearing no clothes.

My task in the following chapters is to explore the threads that connect these two themes (1) in feminist interpretations of the history of philosophy, (2) in feminist debates about theories of knowledge, and (3) in feminist contributions to ethics. I hope by this effort to bring some measure of information to counter the misinformation that is rampant on the corridors of philosophy and to provide a resource to students who are interested in feminist theories that have gained recognition in the international arena of philosophy.

Notes

1. Now that the University of Copenhagen has its first woman rector, one can hope that the university leadership will seek to change this situation.

2. There has been much debate about whether the increase from six to twelve months of maternity leave is in fact women-friendly or whether it will significantly interfere with women's employment opportunities and lifetime earnings. Sweden has a more progressive family-leave policy, which requires fathers to use part of the leave allotted to the family.

3. "Report: U.S. Maternity Plans Pale in Comparison to Other Nations," *Washington Post*, www.chron.com/content/chronicle/nation/98/02/16/maternity leave.2-0.html, 15 February 1998 [accessed 23 August 2002].

4. Anette Borchost, ed. *Kønsmagt under forandring*. (Copenhagen: Hans Reitzels, 2002). Reviewed by Jens Andersen, "Mænd foretrakker stadig mænd," in *Berlingske Tidende*, 8 March 2002, section 2, 2.

5. Nobel prize–winning economist Amartya Sen introduced the phrase "missing women" in the late 1980s, to refer to the 100 million women who were not there because of unusually high mortality rates in certain parts of the world. Here I use the phrase to refer to women who never became philosophers, for lack of educational opportunities and cultural and institutional support.

6. Two books published in the 1980s are especially relevant to this discussion: Mary Field Belenky et al., *Women's Ways of Knowing* (New York:

Basic Books, 1986) and Carol Gilligan, *In a Different Voice* (Cambridge: Harvard University Press, 1982). Note that these books discuss gender differences on the basis of psychological theories of human development (e.g., Nancy Chodorow, *The Reproduction of Mothering* [Berkeley: University of California Press, 1978]), and on the basis of how familial and institutional contexts reproduce gender differences.

7. Luce Irigaray, *An Ethics of Sexual Difference*, trans. Carolyn Burke and Gillian C. Gill (London: Athlone Press, 1993), 5.

8. Judith Butler, *Bodies that Matter* (New York: Routledge, 1993), 22.

9. An article entitled "Et hundeliv" [A Dog's Life] in *Forsker Forum* Nr. 129, November 1999, 10, about "løse ansættelser" (part-time positions) stated: "Der er flere kvinder end mænd, som er villige til at afbryde en forskerkarriere og finde et andet arbejde. . . . Kvinder føler et familieansvar og er mere optagede af at få arbejdsliv og privatliv til at fungere." [There are more women than men who are willing to interrupt a research career and find alternative work. . . . Women feel a family responsibility and are more concerned to make work life function together with private life.] My translation.

10. Maurice Merleau-Ponty emphasized that my concrete existence is always sexual being in *Phenomenology of Perception*, trans. C. Smith (London: Routledge and Kegan Paul, 1962), 156, 182.

11. Lorraine Code, "Taking Subjectivity into Account," in *Feminist Epistemologies*, ed. Elizabeth Potter and Linda Martín Alcoff (New York: Routledge, 1993), 18–19, 39.

12. John Stuart Mill, "The Subjection of Women," in John Stuart Mill and Harriet Taylor Mill, *Essays on Sex Equality*, ed. Alice S. Rossi (Chicago and London: University of Chicago Press, 1970), 215.

13. Mill, 221–35.

14. Simone de Beauvoir, *The Second Sex*, trans. and ed. H. M. Parshley (New York: Vintage Books, 1974), xviii.

15. Elizabeth Grosz, "Contemporary Theories of Power and Subjectivity," in *Feminist Knowledge: Critique and Construct*, ed. Sneja Gunew (London and New York: Routledge, 1990), 60.

16. Penelope Deutscher, *Yielding Gender: Feminism, Deconstruction, and the History of Philosophy* (London and New York: Routledge, 1997), 165–66. I will discuss strategies for reading the "feminine" in the history of philosophy in the next chapter.

17. For example, see Herbert Marcuse, "The Concept of Essence," in *Negations: Essays in Critical Theory*, trans. Jeremy J. Shapiro (Boston: Beacon Press, 1968), 43–87.

18. Martha Nussbaum, *Women and Human Development: The Capabilities Approach* (Cambridge: Cambridge University Press, 2000), 5, 74, 78.

19. Seyla Benhabib, *Situating the Self: Gender, Community, and Postmodernism in Contemporary Ethics* (New York: Routledge, 1992), 2–3.

20. In the next chapter, I will discuss the ways in which philosophers have associated the concepts woman, irrationality, body, and sexuality.

21. Judith Butler, *Bodies that Matter*, 9.

22. Butler, *Bodies*, 10.

23. Butler, *Bodies*, 1.

24. Christine Battersby, *The Phenomenal Woman* (Cambridge and Oxford: Polity Press, 1998), 3.

25. Linda Martín Alcoff, *Real Knowing* (Ithaca: Cornell University Press, 1996), 229.

26. Alcoff and Potter, *Feminist Epistemologies*, 3.

27. *Newsletter Women Philosophers*, no. 3, 8.

28. Susan Neiman, *The Unity of Reason* (New York and Oxford: Oxford University Press, 1994).

29. These questions echo Luce Irigaray's concerns, although Irigaray argues that sexual, not racial, difference is the primary question of the present.

30. See Karl Marx, "Manifesto of the Communist Party," in *The Marx-Engels Reader*, ed. Robert C. Tucker, (New York and London: W. W. Norton and Co., 1978), 469–500. Georg Lukács, "Reification and the Consciousness of the Proletariat," in *History and Class Consciousness: Studies in Marxist Dialectics*, trans. Rodney Livingstone (Cambridge: MIT Press, 1971), 83–222.

31. Alcoff and Potter, *Feminist Epistemologies*, 13.

32. Pierre Bourdieu, *Homo Academicus*, trans. Peter Collier (Cambridge: Polity Press, 1988), 84–90.

33. UN Wire, www.unfoundation.org/unwire [accessed 9 March 2000] and UN Wire, "Women and Population" [accessed 13 March 2000].

~

CHAPTER ONE

Feminism and the
History of Philosophy

Feminist rereadings of the history of philosophy were one of the first fields for the burgeoning new work of feminist philosophy in the early 1970s. After all, philosophers who made up the core canon in Western philosophy were without exception men, most of whom had made reprehensible comments about women. One could open a text of Plato, Aristotle, Rousseau, or Kant and find one's feminist suspicions confirmed: Philosophers *had* been sexist. And should one point out this pattern to fellow students or to teachers, their attitudes merely reinforced this tradition. For their response, still typical today in Denmark, was: "Oh, there she goes again." This response was meant to point out the obvious, that the feminist philosopher or student in question simply did not understand that what Aristotle or Kant wrote about women is wholly irrelevant to their philosophical theories. It may be unfortunate that Kant had written, "I hardly believe that the fair sex is capable of principles," but surely one should ignore this sentiment in dealing with his moral theory. If anything, this example of Kant's historical prejudice buttressed their own confident belief in progress, since none of them would be caught dead writing that "a woman who had a head full of Greek . . . or carries on fundamental controversies about mechanics . . . might as well even have a beard, for perhaps that would express more obviously the mien of profundity for which she strives."[1] (Though they may have their own views about who counted as a real woman.)

So the early attempts to trace the history of what philosophers had written about women located itself on a negative affective range. One faced what the French philosopher Michèle le Doeuff has termed the paradoxes of sexism: "It has all been over since about the day before yesterday, and yet I experience it just this instant."[2] Hence, feminist philosophers sought to use their anger productively in creating new approaches to the history of philosophy.

Since the publication of the first source books, like Mary Ma-howald's *Philosophy of Woman* (1978),[3] the relation between feminism and the history of philosophy has become more nuanced and sophisticated, though no less difficult. How can the terms "feminist" and "history of philosophy" sit comfortably together in one phrase? On the one side, one meets skeptics from the ranks of philosophers. First of all, many philosophers expect to hear a compelling justification for why they should be concerned about the *history* of philosophy at all, instead of just addressing contemporary problems in philosophy. Second, those historians of philosophy who valiantly defend their cause will ask, What does gender have to do with it? What does, e.g., Aristotle's views of women have to do with philosophy? On the other side, from other feminists one meets with skepticism based on a sense of disproportion.[4] How can women's access to, and representation in, philosophy be vital for ongoing emancipatory struggles?

Although I teased with the objection–reply form in the introduction, as if one could supply knockdown arguments for or against feminist philosophy, I do not believe that any argument can provide the final knockout, nor should philosophy set this as its goal. All arguments are based on presuppositions, values, and exclusions that function in the argument in a particular way. It is not my pretension to provide the final convincing argument for the value of the history of philosophy and feminist work in this field and thereby eliminate all further questions. But I will try to show some of the overlapping interests of both critics and defenders of feminist work in the history of philosophy. Instead of presupposing that work in the history of philosophy and in feminism are naturally at odds with each other, and arguing for a postwar pact of reconciliation, I will try to show that the opposite is the case. Feminism helps philosophy do its job better, and feminist work in the history of philosophy is an important contribution to contemporary philosophical work. As Michèle le Doeuff wrote in *Hipparchia's Choice*:

> "thinking philosophically" and "being a feminist" appear as one and the same attitude: a desire to judge by and for oneself. . . . If philosophy particularly consists in questioning what happens in towns, houses and people's daily lives (and, according to Cicero, such is philosophy's task as seen by Socrates), then the issue of women's lives is necessarily on the agenda. But has it really been so, as an issue, in the twenty-five centuries of philosophy that we can observe? Too little or not in the right way, the feminist would say: so here we have an enquiry and a process to be taken further.
>
> For the project of philosophy and that of feminist thinking has a fundamental structure in common, an art of fighting fire with fire and looks with looks, of objectifying and analyzing surrounding thought, of regarding beliefs as objects that must be scrutinized, when the supposedly normal attitude is to submit to what social life erects as doctrine. Nothing goes without saying, including what people think about the roles which have come down to men and women.[5]

And yet, though the most lively philosophical attitude is in harmony with feminism, uniting feminist and philosophical identities in one person still produces a kind of contradiction. And that is because being a philosopher has not been defined strictly in terms of rigorous intellectual inquiry and self-reflection. Instead, being a philosopher has typically carried with it certain aspects of what le Doeuff calls an imaginary. The imaginary dimension of philosophy does not mean that philosophy is unreal. The term "imaginary" brings into focus the theatrical staging of the philosopher's body: the seriousness of the face, a demeanor that focuses on the austerity of thought as opposed to the frivolity of personal grooming. This comportment may help lead a young man with the conviction of the superiority of his own thought onto a path by which he becomes the sage, whom the next generation must simultaneously emulate and surpass.[6] Already one can detect the difficulties for women philosophers, for nowhere in our cultural heritage have we learned that philosophers are young, attractive women

the "face" of philosophy?

wearing shirts that expose their navels, or that philosophers are pregnant, or that they are mothers.

The imaginary focuses as well on certain assumptions about how to write philosophy, which separate those who write "mere commentary" from those who create something "original." In commenting on the different kinds of philosophical writing that one can distinguish in French examination systems, typically linked to the sexes of the candidates, le Doeuff notes

> a paper can be identified as masculine by its authoritative tone, by the way interpretation dominates over receptivity to the text, resulting in a decisive and profound reading or in fantastic misinterpretation. Women, on the other hand, are all receptivity, and their papers are characterized by a kind of polite respect for the fragmentation of the other's discourse (this is called 'acuteness in detailed commentary but lack of overview'). . . . Men treat the text familiarly and knock it about happily; women treat it with a politeness.[7]

And although the latter type of writing may have a number of virtues associated with it, e.g., a nuanced attention to detail or an awareness of gaps in thinking, or it may display a peculiar displacing relation to the text, these types of commentaries are not considered the most authoritative. Hence, women philosophers in France are unlikely to be viewed as the most reliable commentators on a historical text, and their work is rarely used in mainstream courses in the history of philosophy.[8] Thus, texts that display a nonauthoritative style of writing do not become viewed as original philosophical interventions.

A certain style of writing that one can call masculinist, as opposed to male (so as not to identify with it men who refuse to see themselves in this type of imaginary),[9] is one aspect of the philosophical imaginary, as is a certain style of thinking the scope and dimensions of philosophy. Here, one thinks particularly of the presupposition that philosophical work results in a complete philosophical system. This philosophical ideal of systematic completeness has incidentally invoked women as a kind of negative guarantee. For example, in Aristotle's view, woman is characterized by a certain lack of qualities. As le Doeuff writes, "the fact that there is someone (women) incapable of philosophizing is comforting because it shows that philosophy is capable of something." And one of the disturbances of thought created by feminism, which takes up the Socratic injunction to examine one's thoughts up to and beyond the point of discomfort, is to challenge the view that philosophy should even strive for completeness. Instead, the philosophical task must be to retain the notion of the unknown and unthought.[10] So far from refusing the questions raised by feminists to the history of philosophy, it is imperative for philosophers to make known what has been officially excluded, as part of the process of pushing us to the borders of thought.

Canonical Figures and Feminist Questions

There have been many strategies developed to examine the masculinism of the history of philosophy: the investigation of the philosophical imaginary, and of how images used in argumentation distract attention from an argument's gaps or weaknesses; the examination of metaphors used to symbolize the masculine and feminine in philosophy; the focus on how culturally coded qualities of masculinity become identified with shifts in philosophical discourse.[11] All of these strategies, however, thematize the question of how feminists relate to the Western philosophical canon. In one sense, feminist philosophers are using the history of philosophy as other philosophical movements have done, to provide a justification for their contemporary concerns.[12] However, feminist readings are distinguished from nonfeminist readings by an interest in and sensitivity to questions about sexual difference and gender. By way of contrast, consider the following remark by noted American philosopher Richard Rorty: "Each historian of philosophy is working for an 'us' which consists, primarily, of those who see the contemporary philosophical scene as *he* does. So each will treat in a 'witchcraft' manner what another will treat as the antecedents of something real and important in contemporary philosophy."[13] As illustrated by Rorty, the philosophical "us" that reads the history of a philosophy is a "he" that uses gendered terms (e.g., witchcraft) to describe what "he" considers to be bad philosophy. For a feminist historian of philosophy, the problem is how "she" can create a philosophical "us" that includes both women and men, instead of taking "he-ness" as a natural philosophical attribute.

Feminists relate to the Western philosophical canon in a number of ways: First, they may relate negatively to this canon by pointing to the misogyny of philosophers' views of women; the gendered interpretations of theoretical concepts, like matter and form in Aristotle; or the ways in which overarching philosophical concepts of reason and objectivity have been gendered as male, or have arisen out of a world view that is gendered male. By virtue of this critical relation to the Western philosophical canon, feminist philosophers also point out concepts that should be resisted in contemporary theory, and thus the canon functions as a negative resource as well.[14] For example, Elizabeth Spelman's book *Inessential Woman* takes as its starting point a critical assessment of the concept of essence in Platonic philosophy and then uses this vantage point to assess critically how contemporary feminist theorists use the concept "woman."[15]

Second, feminist historians of philosophy may relate to the Western philosophical canon by providing an alternative selection of figures or texts that should be viewed as canonical. This strategy includes the attempt to record the lost voices of women philosophers, as in Mary Ellen Waithe's *A History of Women Philosophers* and the recent series *Re-Reading the Canon*, which upgrades Mary Wollestonecraft, Hannah Arendt, and Simone de Beauvoir to canonical status. Note, however, that the *Encyclopedia of Philosophy*, which contains articles on over nine hundred philosophers, does not have an entry for any of them.[16] By creating an alternative canon, feminist historians of philosophy may be looking for antecedents to issues discussed by contemporary feminist philosophers. This strategy also includes giving renewed attention to male figures in the history of philosophy who often are viewed as marginal (e.g., Anaximander, Heraclitus, Democritus, and Gorgias).[17] Creating an alternative canon may also include developing reading strategies that focus on nonorthodox texts or moments by authors who are firmly established in the canon. The French philosopher Barbara Cassin writes:

> Of course, it turns out that the canonical texts, too, have to be treated in the same fashion. . . . This occurs in their heterodoxical moments, when they are obliged to confront the 'others': witness the extreme dif-

ficulty of book Gamma of Aristotle's Metaphysics or Plato's Sophist. It also appears in the very singularity of the works that are created, torn between denials and inventions.[18]

Third, feminists may turn to the history of philosophy for positive resources that can be an inspiration for addressing contemporary issues that feminist philosophers confront. For example, Martha Nussbaum turns to Aristotle for an understanding of the role of emotion, relationships, and context in ethical life; Moira Gatens and Genevieve Lloyd turn to Spinoza's understanding of the body as "in relation" for a reconceptualization of the imaginary and of the possibility of social inclusion; Annette Baier finds inspiration in David Hume's reflections on moral sentiment and actual moral practices; and Charlene Seigfried argues for the value of pragmatism for contemporary feminism.[19] Other feminists focus on John Stuart Mill's and Friedrich Engels's reflections on the rights and liberties of all individuals—including women—and thus view their works as supportive of contemporary feminist principles.[20]

Before I turn to questions of methodology, I will illustrate the original impetus for feminist work in this field found in the statements made by philosophers about women and femininity.[21] Feminist philosophers have interpreted texts by, e.g., Aristotle and Kant in highly divergent ways, and I will give some examples of these differences.[22]

The statements made by philosophers about women and concepts frequently associated with women, such as the body and emotions, are embroiled in controversy—often a controversy over feminism's core values and theoretical commitments. For example, some feminist philosophers consider Plato's The Republic to be a compelling declaration about the equality of men and women in the guardian class. Yet other feminists call attention to the passages in the Timaeus where Plato describes the creation of women as follows: "Of the men who came into the world, those who were cowards or led unrighteous lives may with reason be supposed to have changed into the nature of women in the second generation. . . . Thus were created women and the female sex in general" (Timaeus 90e–91e).[23] In The Republic, one can find evidence for both generous and critical interpretations of Plato's views on women. For example, in book 5 he explicitly rejects the view that sexual differences influence men's and women's natural capacities to rule.

> If it appears that the male and the female sex have distinct qualifications for any arts or pursuits, we shall affirm that they ought to be assigned respectively to each. But if it appears that they differ only in just this respect that the female bears and the male begets, we shall say that no proof has yet been produced that the woman differs from the man for our purposes, but we shall continue to think that our guardians and their wives ought to follow the same pursuits. (*Republic*, 454d–e)

And yet he immediately qualifies this claim, "women naturally share in all pursuits and men in all—yet, for all the woman is weaker than the man" (*Republic*, 455d–e). Moreover, in book 4, he introduces women in the class of individuals in whom the worse part rules the better. He contrasts "the mob of motley appetites and pleasures and pains one would find chiefly in children and women and slaves and in the base rabble of those who are free men in name" with "the simple and moderate appetites which with the aid of reason and right opinion are guided by consideration" (*Republic* 431c). Elsewhere, he confines the lamentations of grief to women and inferior men and exhorts young men seeking to become "brave, sober, pious, free" (*Republic* 395c) to avoid imitating women. So the controversy about the feminist implications of Plato's texts to a considerable extent revolves about how to situate the egalitarianism of book 5 of *The Republic* in relation to Plato's inegalitarianism, which posits that different natures are rooted in different kinds of souls.[24]

Feminist scholars also disagree about how to understand the most important female figure in the dialogues, namely the priestess Diotima in the *Symposium*, whom Socrates calls his teacher about love. How did Diotima learn about love's true nature and gain philosophical wisdom? Luce Irigaray cautions against taking literally this description of Diotima in the dialogue. Although Socrates cites Diotima's teaching, Irigaray reminds us: "She does not take part in these exchanges or in this meal among men. She is not there. She herself does not speak. . . . And Diotima is not the only example of a woman whose wisdom, especially about love, is reported in her absence by a man."[25] Irigaray's ironic comment about Diotima's absence becomes a starting point for an alternative reading of Diotima's views about love that includes the fecundity of both body and soul.

In reading Aristotle, feminists have debated the relation between his views about human biology and his metaphysical and political concepts. For example, in the *Generation of Animals* Aristotle characterizes the male and female principles by the contrasts between form and matter, active and passive (716b11).[26] Although the female, material principle and the male, formative principle are necessary for reproduction, the female remains inferior to the male. Aristotle writes, "the female, in fact, is female on account of inability of a sort" (728a18). And Aristotle sees these principles not only in physical existence, but in the "mental characteristics of the two sexes" (*History of Animals* 608a21–22). In *Politics* Aristotle also writes, "It is clear that the rule of the soul over the body and of the mind and the rational element over the passionate is natural and expedient; whereas the equality of the two is always hurtful. The same holds good of animals in relation to men. . . . Again, the male is by nature superior, and the female inferior, and the one rules and the other is ruled" (*Politics* 1254b5–15). Commentators who disagree on the value of Aristotle's philosophy for contemporary feminist debates agree that he is sexist. Cynthia Freeland writes,

> Aristotle says that the courage of a man lies in commanding, a woman's lies in obeying; that "matter yearns for form," as the female for the male and the ugly for the beautiful; that women have fewer teeth than men; that a female is an incomplete male or "as it were, a deformity": which contributes only matter and not form to the generation of offspring; that in general "a woman is perhaps an inferior being"; that female characters in tragedy will be inappropriate if they are too brave or too clever.[27]

The question becomes the following: do Aristotle's sexist comments give rise to a gendered interpretation of his metaphysical views?

A gendered interpretation implies that Aristotle's metaphysical concepts are connected either explicitly or implicitly with his views on gender and sexual difference. The argument for a gendered interpretation takes the following form: The hierarchical relation between form and matter provides a conceptual framework that informs most of Aristotle's philosophy, from biology to metaphysics and politics. If form and matter are respectively associated with masculinity and femininity, then one could argue that Aristotle's work is fundamentally "masculinist."[28] Hence, one cannot merely remove Aristotle's theory of sex difference from the rest of his philosophy, because it expresses social values that become the basis for a metaphysics that is politicized and is used to justify the subordination of all women as well as of some men (slaves).[29] Alternatively, those who reject a gendered interpretation argue that the gender associations of matter and form are extrinsic to Aristotle's theory. Although Aristotle's metaphysical framework captures a reality that is already value laden, the fact that maleness became associated with form and femaleness with matter was incidental to his metaphysics as such. This reformist interpretation of Aristotle suggests that gender associations can be removed without undermining his metaphysical theory. For the reformist interpretation, after removing the gender associations from Aristotle's metaphysics, one can use his theory of substance as a positive resource for the present by pointing to the underlying relation between normative values and description.[30]

Feminist philosophers have also highlighted what key thinkers in the Christian tradition have written about women and the feminine. St. Augustine's texts express the view that women are more closely linked to the corrupt body than men, making their subordination both natural and commendable. He writes, "There is nothing I am more determined to avoid than relations with a woman. I feel that there is nothing which so degrades the high intelligence of a man than the embraces of a woman and the contact with her body, without which it is impossible to possess a wife."[31] And in the *Confessions* he writes,

> And just as in man's soul there are two forces, one which is dominant because it deliberates and one which obeys because it is subject to such guidance, in the same way, in the physical sense, woman has been made for man. In her mind and her rational intelligence she has a nature the equal of man's, but in sex she is physically subject to him in the same way as our natural impulses need to be subjected to the reasoning power of the mind, in order that the actions to which they lead may be inspired by the principles of good conduct. (13.32.344)

In Augustine's view, the subjugation of woman to man incarnates the spiritual hierarchy that man must strive to achieve within his own soul. In insisting on both women's rational equality and physical subordination, Augustine suggests that women experience a split between their rational soul and their embodied existence that men do not experience.[32] Hence, Genevieve Lloyd argues, "despite this conscious upgrading of female nature, his own interpretations still put women in an ambivalent position with respect to Reason."[33]

Augustine's dual conception of women's spiritual and physical being leads him to attribute conflicting qualities to women's nature. He writes, "A good Christian is found in one and the same woman to love the creature of God whom he desires to be transformed and renewed, but to hate in her the corruptible and moral conjugal connection, sexual intercourse and all that pertains to her as wife."[34] Although women were created for the purpose of aiding in generation, Augustine argues that after resurrection, this function will be transcended. Women's bodies will retain their "nature," not their "vice"; they shall be "superior to carnal intercourse and child-bearing."[35] Thus, the resurrection of women's true nature negates the function for which they were created in earthly existence.

Thus, Augustine's views about women are inconsistent, maintaining both women's social and political *inequality* and their *equality* in the "City of God." As Penelope Deutscher argues in *Yielding Gender*, the issue for feminist theorists is what methodologies can be used to interpret such inconsistencies in the history of philosophy.[36] Should the ambivalence in these texts be pardoned in light of the relative progress Augustine's views represents over those of the other Church Fathers? Are there alternative methodological strategies to interpret the ambivalence in these texts? I will return to these questions of methodology below.

Thomas Aquinas problematizes the very creation of women in *Summa Theologica*. He poses the question of "whether woman should have been made in the first production of things."[37] Aquinas suggests that woman's existence is problematic because, as Aristotle says, she is a "misbegotten male," because she is naturally subjugated to man, and because she is the occasion for sin. If God's creation is in all respects good, it is puzzling to Aquinas how such an imperfect being as woman could have been made in this original act of production. Thus, Aquinas explains women's role in the following terms: "It was necessary for a woman to be made, as the Scripture says, as *a helper* to man; not, indeed, as a helpmate in other works, as some say, since man can be more efficiently helped by another man in other works; but as a helper in the work of generation (*ST* 1.92.1). As to the question of why sexual differentiation is at all necessary for human biology, Aquinas's answer is that sexual differentiation allows for a separation across the sexes between the active and passive powers in generation, which makes possible man's pursuance of the noble, "vital operation" of intellection. Aquinas reinforces this identification of male with the operations of reason when he claims that man serves as the "principle" of human existence. He writes, "As God is the principle of the whole universe, so the first man, in likeness to God, was the principle of the whole human race" (*ST* 1.92.2). If man is the principle of the human race, then he must contain all the perfections of human existence. Since reason is the noblest function of human existence, intellectual operations must be contained in this first principle of the human race.

Although women are necessary to carry out the work of generation and to provide the precondition for man's pursuit of intellectual activity, her sex is also a flaw. Aquinas notes that the production of woman stems from a defect in the active force that produces man. This defect may be caused by internal deficiencies, or by external interferences such as a moist south wind (*ST* 1.92.1). Woman is indispensable for serving the end of nature in general but misbegotten as an individual. Woman's deficiency is manifested in her comparatively greater affinity with the passions and in her weaker affinity with reason. In the *Supplement* to the *Summa Theologica*, Aquinas writes, "In women the humors are more abundant, wherefore they are more inclined to be led by their concupiscences."[38] In comparison, "A man has more of the good of reason, which prevails over all movements of bodily passions" (*Supplement* 62.4). Because of women's inclination to be led by passion, marriage cannot be a relationship between equals, but is one of "proportional" equality (*Supplement* 64.5). Aquinas compares this proportional equality between husband and wife to the complementary relation between active and passive elements. And he argues that woman's subjection to man existed even before the fall:

"woman is naturally subject to man, because in man the discretion of reason predominates" (*ST* 1.92.1).

Thus, Aquinas presents an ambiguous picture of women's relation to reason. On the one hand, he attributes to her an intellectual soul that is the image of God and is itself without sexual differentiation: "The image of God belongs to both sexes, since it is in the mind, wherein there is no distinction of sexes" (*ST* 1.93.6). On the other hand, Aquinas persists in claiming that in a secondary sense, the image of God is found only in man and not in woman: "For man is the beginning and end of woman; as God is the beginning and end of every creature" (*ST* 1.93.4). For feminist philosophers, the question is not whether Aquinas's writings express sexist sentiments. More significantly, the question is whether his ideals of reason themselves carry a gendered meaning. As Genevieve Lloyd has argued, although woman does not symbolize for Aquinas an inferior form of rationality, because woman's meaning is bound up with reproduction, she is "symbolically located outside the actual manifestations of Reason within human life." Hence, more is at stake in Aquinas's texts than a "succession of surface misogynist attitudes within philosophical thought. It is not a question simply of the applicability to women of neutrally specified ideas of rationality, but rather of the genderization of the ideals themselves."[39]

Although one could continue discussing the philosophical implications of texts in the Western philosophical canon that explicitly address women's nature, it is not my project to provide a complete resource to the reader. I merely have pointed to some of the examples that have been a reference point for feminist historians of philosophy. Hence, I will include only one more philosopher in this section, Immanuel Kant, who has been a focal point for my own work in the feminist history of philosophy.

Kant's comments on women are hardly a positive testimony to the progressive character of the Enlightenment project articulated by Kant. Kant considers woman's character, in contrast to man's, to be wholly defined by natural needs. He writes, "Nature was concerned about the preservation of the embryo and implanted fear into the woman's character, a fear of physical injury and a timidity toward similar dangers. On the basis of this weakness, the woman legitimately asks for masculine protection."[40] Because of their natural fear and timidity, women are viewed as unsuited for scholarly work. Kant mockingly describes the scholarly women who "use their books somewhat like a watch, that is, they wear the watch so it can be noticed that they have one, although it is usually broken or does not show the correct time" (*Anthropology*, 221). And in his view, women's philosophy is "not to reason, but to sense."[41] No wonder that under these conditions the woman "makes no secret in wishing that she might rather be a man, so that she could give larger and freer latitude to her inclinations; no man, however, would want to be a woman (*Anthropology*, 222). Although one might be tempted to dismiss Kant's misogynist views as merely a reflection of an earlier epoch, Kant himself was exposed to more progressive views. The lawyer Theodor von Hippel, mayor of Königsberg and friend of Kant, was a spokesperson for equal human and civil rights for women.

Because of Kant's misogyny and his apparent disdain for the body, Kant is the modern philosopher that feminists find most objectionable.[42] However, many feminists seek to redefine the ground on which a sympathetic dialogue with Kant can be found.[43] These competing views are generated about Kant's categorical imperative, which he at one point formulates as "I should never act in such a way that I could not also will my maxim should be a universal law."[44] Kant's moral philosophy demands respect for persons as rational beings, warns against treating persons as means to an end, and argues against any role for emotion in ethical judgment except the feeling of respect for the moral law. Some feminist philosophers have argued that Kant's formalist conception of the moral law is based on a false dichotomy between reason and nature and cannot be adequate to understanding the complexities of human life.[45] Other feminist philosophers argue that Kant's formal rule of morality is both universalist and radically individualizing, and that Kant's ethics can be an important tool in identifying the wrongs to which women are subjected because of their gender.[46]

Kant's aesthetic reflections in the *Critique of Judgment* have been central for contemporary resurgence of interest in Kant. In this text, Kant moves away from the mechanistic conception of nature that is dominant in the *Critique of Pure Reason* and emphasizes the harmonious interplay of the imagination and understanding, which gives rise to the experience of objects *as if* they were designed for our own purposes. In a sympathetic feminist account, one philosopher argues that Kant's notion of common sense—*sensus communis*—opens up the possibility not just of thinking with others, but of feeling with others, and thus creates a space for imagination and feeling that revises Kant's earlier account of moral subjectivity.[47] In a critical feminist account, another philosopher argues that Kant's theory about the beautiful and the sublime continues the long list of dualisms in Western culture, including the dualisms between form/matter, mind/body, reason/emotion, transcendent/immanent, all of which have a gendered meaning in Western civilization.[48]

Similarly, there are competing interpretations by feminist philosophers of Kant's rationalism. For example, in my book *Cognition and Eros: A Critique of the Kantian Paradigm*, I focused on reason's role in scientific knowledge and on the cognitive relation between the knower and the object of knowledge.[49] In Kant's formalistic conception of knowledge, he treats observation as paradigmatic for knowing, and thus excludes awareness of our own sensory involvement with the object of knowledge. In excluding feeling from knowledge, even from knowledge of oneself, Kant develops a cognitive corollary to his earlier views that compare emotions and passions to "an illness of mind because both emotion and passion, exclude the sovereignty of reason" (*Anthropology*, 73, 155). Moreover, the abstract nature of the "I think" that accompanies all knowledge indicates that the subject does not develop or change through the process of knowing. And the role of a priori concepts of the understanding, which are prior to and independent of experience, leads to a conception of knowledge that is impervious to any historical changes in relations between subjects and objects of knowledge. Hence, I argue that Kant's philosophy illustrates an ascetic posture that is based on a distancing from and denigration of feeling, sensuality, and the feminine.

Other feminist philosophers offer a more positive reading of the formal features of Kant's epistemology. The black American philosopher Adrian Piper focuses on the resources available in Kant's conception of the self for knowing other persons.[50] Piper takes up the question of xenophobia, which she defines as "a fear of individuals who violate one's empirical conception of persons and so one's self-conception."[51]

She asks, What is it that prevents one from recognizing a particular third-person other as a person? And can one correct for this exclusion of a particular empirical other from personhood? Piper argues that Kant's theory of the self provides for the possibility of correcting against xenophobia. Even though an individual might have an empirically limited conception of persons (e.g., they may not have wide acquaintance with blacks), since reason works to enlarge our understanding by searching for further data by which to explain it, then the rational subject welcomes new experiences as cognitive challenges. Piper concludes that the Kantian self not only has the resources for correcting for xenophobia, but it can even be characterized by a kind of xenophilia, "a positive valuation of human difference as intrinsically interesting . . . and a disvaluation of conformity to one's honorific stereotypes as intrinsically uninteresting."[52]

Although feminist rereadings of the history of Western philosophy were motivated initially by the desire to analyze critically philosophical misogyny, these interpretations have had much more encompassing results. They have led to a rethinking of themes within ethics, aesthetics, epistemology, and metaphysics. Though there is no one feminist way of reading a particular philosopher, there are certain common threads in these interpretations. Feminist philosophers raise questions about embodiment, emotion, imagination, community, and power relations. Feminist interpretations are guided by an ethical interest as well, as they explore the ways in which philosophical theories either sustain a logic of domination or provide resources to resist such a logic.

Methodological Reflections

Although feminist work in the history of philosophy began with what one might now consider banal recitations of misogynist comments on women, it has developed into a field that is reflective about methodology in a way that contributes to making the field of the history of philosophy profoundly philosophical.[53] Feminist philosophers do not now pose the question, "is Plato or Aristotle or Kant sexist?" Rather, they analyze the range of affective, conceptual, and institutional issues that mediate both women's and men's relation to the history of philosophy. Affective issues may include questions such as: Does the reader relate to the text through anger or through pleasure? How does the position and content of imagery in an argument produce the effect of conviction? Conceptual issues include questions about knowledge, ethics, politics, or aesthetics, as well as methodological questions about how to interpret texts. Institutional issues include questions about how certain forms of commentary are viewed as authoritative and other kinds of commentary are viewed as nonauthoritative because of their maverick nature, about how certain topics of research are viewed as legitimate for professional philosophers and students while other topics are excluded as illegitimate.[54]

In the beginning of this chapter I referred to three classifications for feminist work in the history of philosophy. (1) A *negative* relation to the canon includes approaches that focus on the misogyny of a philosopher, on gendered interpretations of specific concepts, and on gendered interpretations of overarching themes in the history of philosophy. (2) An *alternative canon* consists in revisions about which writers and texts should be included in the canon of the history of philosophy. (3) A *positive relation* to the philosophical canon emphasizes how feminists inherit resources from this tradition that are productive for contemporary feminist concerns. Although this classification is useful, it does hold the danger of oversimplification. What about interpretations that express more than one of these ways of relating to the canon, or none of them? For example, the strategies of reading history of philosophy inspired by deconstruction do not fit neatly into this classification. As Penelope Deutscher argues in *Yielding Gender*, the unstable or contradictory character of concepts such as reason, male, female, and human has the effect of sustaining a phallocentric argument in a text. In this sense, deconstructive feminism has a negative or critical relation to canonical texts. But deconstructionism also makes a more general claim, that philosophical writing is saturated with tensions and ambivalences, despite textual claims for rational consistency and completeness. Thus, for deconstructionist feminism, the interesting question is not, Do feminists relate to the history of philosophy negatively or positively? but rather, What methodological contributions do feminists make in reading the history of philosophy?

Methodologically, feminist philosophers have chosen various strategies for interpreting how the terms "masculinity" and "femininity" are used in an ambiguous or contradictory fashion in philosophical texts. One strategy is to argue that *despite* the uneven statements of thinkers like St. Augustine or Jean-Jacques Rousseau, the masculine connotations of reason prevail. For example, in *The Man of Reason* Genevieve Lloyd argues that *despite* the complexity of Rousseau's view of the relation between nature and reason, he excludes women from a concept of reason that has a masculine association. A second strategy is to argue that the complexity and contradiction within a thinker like Rousseau *mitigates* or *diminishes* the misogyny of the text. Deutscher draws from deconstruction a third strategy for reading contradictions. She criticizes both these two approaches for having the effect of making the text more consistent or stable than it actually is. She writes, "Feminist philosophy also needs to focus on contradictory textual tendencies, rather than looking between or beyond them to the 'real meaning' of a confused philosophical argument, or looking behind them, as when critics think such tendencies are trivial, or attempt to explain or account for them."[55] Therefore, she asks: what are the effects of contradictions in a text? Her thesis is that the phallocentric alignment of reason and humanity with masculinity can be sustained *because* of these contradictions and ambiguities.

At least three prominent French women philosophers have focused on textual instability: Michèle le Doeuff, Sara Kofman, and Luce Irigaray. Michèle le Doeuff, as noted earlier, works with the imagery in philosophical arguments. She describes her work as being "about the stock of images you can find in philosophical works, whatever they refer to: insects, clocks, women, or islands. I try to show what part they play in the philosophical enterprise."[56] Le Doeuff analyzes how textual elements that appear as strictly marginal in a philosophical work have the effect of concealing or substituting for problems in the argument. She writes, "The perspective I am adopting here . . . involves reflecting on strands of the imaginary operating in places where in principle, they are supposed not to belong and yet where, without them, nothing would have been accomplished."[57] Thus, le Doeuff analyzes the rhetoric in a philosophical text by looking at points of weakness and contradictions in an argument.

Sara Kofman's readings of Nietzsche, Freud, Comte, Kant, and Rousseau, draw on a methodology that she considers to be both deconstructive and psychoanalytical. She focuses on the distinction between what texts purport to do and what they really do. For example, she interprets Rousseau's use of the term "respect" for women as a symptom of a complex structure of ambivalence toward women. And she looks at how Rousseau's contradictions about women are functional for his text. But at the same time, she offers a causal explanation for these contradictions, e.g., by looking at the author's unconscious intent. In this respect, Kofman's emphasis is on what motivates the contradictory logic in a philosopher rather than on what this logic enables in the text.

Of these three French philosophers, Luce Irigaray most systematically explores the logic of instability. For Irigaray, the representations of masculine and feminine are themselves generated by a paradoxical structure. Her hypothesis is that "woman" has always been defined as the necessary complement to, or negative image of, masculinity in philosophy. Women have been represented only in terms that are relational to a masculine reference. Therefore, Irigaray's project is to analyze how a text does *not represent women*. She argues that philosophy has the power to "reduce all others to the economy of the Same" and "eradicate the difference between the sexes."[58] And thus Irigaray's thesis is that the concept of femininity is a possibility that is both outside and inside the borders of philosophy. The concept of femininity is outside the history of philosophy, since the representation of women has been excluded from philosophy. But the concept of femininity is not entirely outside, since philosophy gestures toward it as an excluded possibility. Hence, the concept of femininity has a paradoxical inside–outside structure, and representations of the masculine and the feminine are themselves an effect of this structural ambivalence. Irigaray's strategy for reading texts in the history of philosophy shows how the contradictions implicit in these terms have the effect of sustaining the phallocentric premises of the text.

These three authors use the analysis of textual instability to point to negative features in the philosophical canon, i.e., they show how contradictions sustain phallocentricism. In this sense they exemplify a "disinvestment approach"—i.e., they do not take ownership of this philosophical tradition, as philosophers who invoke the inheritance model do, since they see in this tradition the perpetuation of relations of domination. Nor do they abandon philosophy. Since the philosophical tradition cannot be a straightforward resource, they use unorthodox techniques of reading to return uneasily to the house of philosophy.[59] But Michèle le Doeuff also has contributed significantly to building an "alternative" to the canonical texts, e.g., through her substantial work on Simone de Beauvoir. And Luce Irigaray is also deeply inspired by the work of Emmanuel Levinas, as is evident in her book *An Ethics of Sexual Difference*, and thus she uses the history of philosophy for its positive resource as well. Therefore, instead of highlighting negative, positive, or alternative relations to the canon, their work illustrates how methodological innovation in interpreting texts can cut across these categorizations.

Authors who focus on textual instability work with the complexity of a text. But does the deconstructionist focus on textual effects live up to its promise of having an ethical and political dimension? The ethical–political dimension of marxist-inspired readings is more transparent. If conceptual contradictions point to contradictions in social relations, then an analysis of philosophical writing becomes a tool for social critique.[60] But deconstruction explicitly rejects a reference to the extratextual terrain. Derrida writes, "Reading . . . cannot legitimately transgress toward something other than it, toward a referent (a reality that is metaphysical, historical, psychobiographical, etc.)."[61] Can ethical or political intervention occur strictly by pointing to the textual level? Arguably, Irigaray's readings in the history of philosophy give one example of how textual intervention can have ethical effects. She uses irony, humor, mimicry, and parody to subvert the prevalent readings of Plato, Descartes, and other philosophers and to explore the fecundity of sexual difference.[62] Feminist deconstruction also needs to clarify the scope of its strategy. Can feminist deconstruction be applied to all texts within the history of philosophy, even texts that do not address explicitly questions of women and femininity? Or is it focused exclusively on contradictions surrounding gender? If the latter, it could be argued that feminist deconstruction limits feminist readings in the history of philosophy to a narrow domain.

In the preceding section, I have focused on the methodological innovations engendered by a deconstructionist approach to texts. But feminist historians of philosophy also address the standard methodological issues of the field and debate the following questions: Is the task of the (feminist) historian of philosophy to be primarily a *historian*, i.e., to tell it like it was and study the history of philosophy on its own terms? Or is the task of the (feminist) historian of philosophy to use the resources of the history of philosophy to address the *philosophical* issues?[63] The *historical* approach to texts is limited because it presumes that it is possible to be a neutral historian with no specific interest in a text. Feminist historians of philosophy are often critical of this reading practice because it rejects using one's specific interest in the present, e.g., an interest in gender, as an interpretative tool. Moreover, the claim for neutrality in the history of philosophy often accompanies practices of selective focus and thus raises serious doubts about this ideal of neutrality. The *philosophical* approach to texts uses the history of philosophy as inspiration for seeking truths or at least as solutions to current problems or puzzles. Among feminist historians of philosophy, this approach characterizes feminists who view the history of philosophy as an inheritance that can be mined for contemporary feminist concerns. Yet this approach also makes a number of problematic assumptions: that the history of philosophy is primarily a positive resource rather than a negative inheritance; that history is sufficiently continuous so that past truths can address present problems; and that philosophy's goal is to further progress toward truth. Cynthia Freeland suggests a third approach, invoking a pragmatist vision of history of philosophy as an ongoing project of explaining puzzles, rather than as a quest for true views or arguments.[64] This approach recognizes that the resources of the past are always a mixed bag, and that they cannot provide justifications for present views; but these past resources are potentially stimulating for reflection on the present. Feminist pragmatism in reading the history of philosophy incorporates analyses of the context of historical texts, of the values or interests that guide (feminist) research in the present, and is critical of claims for progress in truth without giving up claims for epistemic superiority.

How then do feminist debates contribute to methodological reflections on the history of Western philosophy? For one thing, these debates show that approaches to the history of philosophy that *exclude* feminist questions are themselves ideological, both because they are epistemologically flawed and because they contribute to the justification of social relations of dominance. Feminist philosophers do not claim that all work in the history of philosophy should be guided by questions of gender and sexuality. But they protest against the view that philosophy can interrogate all of the fundamental issues of human life except the fact that humans are both male and female, and how these differences have been sedimented in social, cultural, and intellectual history.

One can detect a shift among feminist commentators from an early negative interest in the philosophical canon to a more recent positive interest. In an interview published in 2000, Genevieve Lloyd commented, "The positive and negative approaches can both be seen as reflecting a feminist perspective on the history of philosophy, but they're very different in spirit. I'm now much more interested in the positive appropriations—in looking *to* sources in the philosophical tradition for ways of reconceptualizing issues that are under current debate, and for ways of opening up our imaginations to alternative ways of thinking, than I am in the more negative criticisms of past philosophers."[65] Penelope Deutscher speculates that this turn to a more positive relation to the history of Western philosophy should be explained not just in intellectual terms, but in affective terms as well. Women philosophers are interested in the practice of philosophy and ask: What does philosophy enable us to be? What affective range does it allow us to occupy? How can one find surprise, pleasure, and humor in the text? In discussing the work of contemporary French women philosophers, Deutscher articulates the questions they implicitly pose to philosophy: "Not just, what can we know, but what range of emotions, stances, and actions does it allow us to occupy? Does it expand our subjective possibilities as negative critics, or as lovers of the new, for example the new that we find amongst the letter of the old? Could feminism engage in a therapeutic assessment of its relationship to the history of philosophy?"[66]

There is no consensus on methodology by feminists who work in the history of philosophy. They work with methodologies that draw on inheritance models, ideology-critique, deconstructionism, psychoanalysis, and pragmatist views; nor should this be understood as an exhaustive account of feminist methodologies. But the multiplicity of approaches does not imply that anything goes. Feminist philosophers are good scholars who contribute subtle, nuanced, and innovative readings. Feminist philosophers generally acknowledge that they participate in a collaborative project and that no one individual interpretation or approach can be final and complete. This spirit of collaboration implies that feminist scholars do not merely tolerate other methods, since the notion of toleration retains the presumption that one's own methodology is the yardstick by which all others should be measured. Rather, feminist debates issue in a perspectivism that acknowledges that differing approaches to history are productive in very different ways. But amidst this diversity, feminist historians of philosophy are animated by the spirit of living the present critically. As the French philosopher Francoise Dastur says in her reading of Heidegger's Rectorat address of 1933, "To be in one's time . . . is to resist one's time, to be in one's time in a critical fashion, out of phase."[67] And since one cannot be utopian about the present, it is in the spirit of living the present critically that feminist readers open up places for innovative readings, dissenting views, and maverick approaches.

Notes

1. Immanuel Kant, *Observations on the Feeling of the Beautiful and Sublime*, trans. John T. Goldthwait (Berkeley: University of California Press, 1960), 132–33, 78.

2. Michèle le Doeuff, *Hipparchia's Choice: An Essay Concerning Women, Philosophy, Etc.*, trans. Trista Selous (Oxford, UK: Blackwell, 1991), 6.

3. Mary Mahowald, ed., *Philosophy of Woman: Classical to Current Concepts* (Indianapolis: Hackett Publishing Co., 1978).

4. Le Doeuff, 5.

5. Le Doeuff, 29.

6. Le Doeuff, 31, 156.

7. Le Doeuff, "Women and Philosophy" in *French Feminist Thought*, ed. Toril Moi (Oxford: Basil Blackwell, 1987), 204–5.

8. Penelope Deutscher, "A Matter of Affect, Passion and Heart: Our Taste for New Narratives of the History of Philosophy," Introduction to *Hypatia*,

Special Issue: Contemporary French Women Philosophers, ed. Penelope Deutscher, vol. 15, no. 4, Fall 2000, 1–17.

9. Le Doeuff, *Hipparchia's Choice*, 139.

10. Le Doeuff, "Women and Philosophy," 193, 209.

11. See, for example, Michèle le Doeuff, *The Philosophical Imaginary*, trans. Colin Gordon (London: Athlone Press, 1989); Genevieve Lloyd, *The Man of Reason: "Male" and "Female" in Western Philosophy* (Minneapolis: University of Minnesota Press, 1984); Susan R. Bordo, *The Flight to Objectivity: Essays on Cartesianism and Culture* (Albany: State University of New York Press, 1987); and Susan Bordo, ed., *Feminist Interpretations of René Descartes* (University Park: The Pennsylvania State University Press, 1999).

12. See Charlotte Witt, "How Feminism is Re-writing the Philosophical Canon," The Alfred P. Stiernotte Memorial Lecture in Philosophy at Quinnipac College, October 2, 1996, www.uh.edu/~cfreelan/SWIP.

13. *Philosophy in History*, ed. Richard Rorty, J. B. Schneewind, Quentin Skinner (Cambridge: Cambridge University Press, 1984), 7, cited in Witt, 1.

14. Witt, 3. See also Cynthia Freeland's "Feminism, Ideology, and Interpretation in Ancient Philosophy," *Apeiron*, vol. 33, no. 4 (December 2000), 365–406.

15. Elizabeth V. Spelman, *Inessential Woman: Problems of Exclusion in Feminist Thought* (Boston: Beacon Press, 1988).

16. Witt, 7. See Mary Ellen Waithe, *A History of Women Philosophers* (Boston: Kluwer Academic Publishers, 1989) and Nancy Tuana, General Editor, *Re-reading the Canon* (University Park: The Pennsylvania State University Press, 1994).

17. Deutscher, 5.

18. Quoted in Deutscher, 6.

19. Witt, 9. Martha Nussbaum, *Love's Knowledge: Essays on Philosophy and Literature* (Oxford: Oxford University Press, 1990); Susan James interviews Genevieve Lloyd and Moira Gatens, "The Power of Spinoza: Feminist Conjunctions" in *Hypatia, Special Issue: Going Australian: Reconfiguring Feminism and Philosophy*, ed. Christine Battersby, Catherine Constable, Rachel Jones, and Judy Purdom, vol. 15, no. 2, Spring 2000, 40–58; Annette Baier, *Postures of the Mind; Essays on Mind and Morals* (Minneapolis: University of Minnesota Press, 1985); Charlene Haddock Seigfried, *Pragmatism and Feminism* (Chicago: University of Chicago Press, 1996). I will discuss the turn toward a positive orientation to the history of philosophy at the end of this chapter.

20. See Mary Briody Mahowald, *Philosophy of Woman: An Anthology of Classic and Current Concepts* (Indianapolis: Hackett Publishing, 1983).

21. There are significant resources for this discussion. I have already mentioned Genevieve Lloyd's *The Man of Reason* and the series *Re-reading the Canon*. I can also recommend Vigdis Songe-Møller, *Den græske drømmen om kvinnens overflødighet. Essays om myter og filosofi i antikkens Hellas* (Oslo: Cappelon Akademisk Forlag, 1999; English translation: *Philosophy without Women; The Birth of Sexism in Western Thought*, London: Continuum, 2003); Mary Wollestonecraft, *A Vindication of the Rights of Woman* (Buffalo, N.Y.: Prometheus Books, 1989), for her comments on Rousseau; Penelope Deutscher, *Yielding Gender: Feminism, Deconstruction and the History of Philosophy* (London: Routledge, 1997), with sections on St. Augustine and Rousseau; Christine Battersby, *The Phenomenal Women: Feminist Metaphysics and the Patterns of Identity* (Cambridge: Polity Press, 1998), with sections on Kant, Hegel, Kierkegaard, and Adorno; and Nancy Tuana, *The Less Noble Sex: Scientific, Religious and Philosophical Conceptions of Women's Nature* (Bloomington: Indiana University Press, 1993), as well as Irigaray's provocative interpretations in *Speculum of the Other Woman*, trans. Gillian C. Gill (Ithaca, N.Y.: Cornell University Press, 1985) and *An Ethics of Sexual Difference*, trans. Carolyn Burke and Gillian C. Gill (London: The Athlone Press, 1993).

22. In the following discussion, I will draw on my own work in *Cognition and Eros: A Critique of the Kantian Paradigm* (Boston: Beacon Press, 1983), especially chapters 1, 3, 4, and 8.

23. Plato, *The Collected Dialogues of Plato including the Letters*, ed. Edith Hamilton and Huntington Cairns (Princeton, N.J.: Princeton University Press, 1961).

24. Elizabeth Spelman, *Inessential Woman*, 25–26.

25. Luce Irigaray, *An Ethics of Sexual Difference*, 20. For an alternative interpretation of Diotima's role, see, for example, Andrea Nye in "Irigaray and Diotima at Plato's Symposium," *Feminist Interpretations of Plato*, ed. Nancy Tuana. See also Martha Nussbaum's reading of the dialogue, which emphasizes the importance of Alcibiades' speech in "The Speech of Alcibiades: A Reading of Plato's *Symposium*," *Philosophy and Literature* 3 (Fall 1979), 131–72.

26. Aristotle, *The Generation of Animals*, trans. A. L. Peck, Loeb Classical Library (Cambridge, Mass.: Harvard University Press, 1942). The citations to other texts refer to *The Basic Works of Aristotle*, ed. Richard McKeon (New York: Random House, 1941).

27. Cynthia Freeland, "Nourishing Speculation: A Feminist Reading of Aristotelian Science," in *Engendering Origins: Critical Feminist Readings in Plato and Aristotle*, ed. Bat-Ami Bar On (Albany: State University of New York Press, 1994), 145–46.

28. For this discussion, see Witt, 4–5.

29. See Elizabeth V. Spelman, "Aristotle and the Politicization of the Soul" in *Discovering Reality: Feminist Perspectives on Epistemology, Metaphysics, Methodology, and Philosophy of Science*, ed. Sandra Harding and Merrill B. Hintikka (Boston: D. Reidel, 1983), 17–30.

30. Witt, 5.

31. *Soliloquia* I.10.17, quoted in Kari Elisabeth Børresen, *Subordination and Equivalence: The Nature and Role of Woman in Augustine and Thomas Aquinas*, 7, trans. Charles H. Talbot (Washington, D.C.: University Press of America, 1981).

32. Børresen, 27.

33. Lloyd, *The Man of Reason*, 29.

34. Quoted in Rosemary Radford Ruether, "Mysogynism and Virginal Feminism in the Fathers of the Church," in *Religion and Sexism*, ed. Rosemary Radford Ruether (New York: Simon and Schuster, 1974), 161.

35. St. Augustine, *The City of God*, trans. Marcus Dods (New York: Random House, 1950), 22.17.839.

36. Deutscher, *Yielding Gender*, 145.

37. Thomas Aquinas, *Summa Theologica*, (*ST*) trans. the Fathers of the English Dominican Province (New York: Benzinger Bros. Inc., 1947), vol. 1, part 1, question 92.

38. *ST* 3, *Supplement*, question 62, article 4.

39. Lloyd, 36–37.

40. Kant, *Anthropology from a Pragmatic Point of View*, 219.

41. Kant, *Anthropology*, 132–33.

42. Barbara Herman, "Could It Be Worth Thinking About Kant on Sex and Marriage?" in *A Mind of Her Own*, ed. Louise Antony and Charlotte Witt (Boulder, Colo.: Westview Press, 1993), 50.

43. For examples of some of these competing views, see my article "Kant," in *A Companion to Feminist Philosophy*, ed. Alison M. Jaggar and Iris Marion Young (Oxford: Blackwell, 1998) and my anthology *Feminist Interpretations of Immanuel Kant* (University Park: Pennsylvania State University Press, 1997). For a Kantian-inspired approach to feminist philosophy, see also Herta Nagl-Docekal, *Feministische Philosophie: Ergebnisse, Probleme, Perspektiven* (Frankfurt am Main: Fischer Taschenbuch Verlag, 2000).

44. Kant, *Foundations of the Metaphysics of Morals*, trans. Lewis White Beck (New York: Macmillan, 1963), 18.

45. Sally Sedgwick, "Can Kant's Ethics Survive the Feminist Critique?" in *Feminist Interpretations of Immanuel Kant*, ed. Robin May Schott.

46. Herta Nagl-Docekal, "Feminist Ethics: How It Could Benefit from Kant's Moral Philosophy," in *Feminist Interpretations of Immanuel Kant*, ed. Schott.

47. Jane Kneller, "The Aesthetic Dimension of Kantian Autonomy," in *Feminist Interpretations of Immanuel Kant*, ed. Schott. See also Marcia Moen's analysis of intersubjectivity in the *Critique of Judgment*, in "Feminist Themes in Unlikely Places: Re-Reading Kant's *Critique of Judgment*" in the same volume.

48. Cornelia Klinger, "The Concepts of the Sublime and the Beautiful in Kant and Lyotard," in *Feminist Interpretations of Immanuel Kant*, ed. Schott. Another critical view is offered by Kim Hall, "*Sensus Communis* and Violence: A Feminist Reading of Kant's *Critique of Judgment*" in the same volume.

49. Today I would no longer argue that Kant's analysis of reason's role in scientific knowledge is paradigmatic for all of the tasks of reason. Instead, I am persuaded by Susan Neiman's interpretation of Kant in *The Unity of Reason* (Oxford: Oxford University Press, 1994), which focuses on Kant's analysis of reason beyond the limits of the cognitive. From this point of view, rationality for Kant is not centrally concerned with the cognitive, but with the unity of theoretical and practical reason and the primacy of practical reason within this unity.

50. Adrian M. S. Piper, "Xenophobia and Kantian Rationalism," in *Feminist Interpretations of Immanuel Kant*, ed. Schott, 21–73.

51. Piper, 48.

52. Piper, 66.

53. Freeland, "Feminism and Ideology in Ancient Philosophy," *Apeiron: A Journal for Ancient Philosophy and Science*, vol. 33, no. 4 (December 2000), 370.

54. See Deutscher, "A Matter of Affect, Passion and Heart" as well as "'Imperfect Discretion': Interventions into the History of Philosophy by Twentieth-Century French Women Philosophers," in *Hypatia, Special Issue: Going Australian: Reconfiguring Feminism and Philosophy*, ed. Christine Battersby, Catherine Constable, Rachel Jones, and Judy Purdom, vol. 15, no. 2, Spring 2000, 160–180. Deutscher argues that the distinction between commentary and originality is a feminist issue, since it fails to identify as original the philosophy that women have written in letters, treatises on education and theology, and commentary on the history of philosophy. For Deutscher the question is "what practices preclude women from being identified as original and innovative philosophers?" (165).

55. Deutscher, 7–8.

56. Cited in Deutscher, 60–61.

57. Cited in Deutscher, 60. Deutscher notes, however, that there is a second strain in le Doeuff's analysis, which leans toward a causal or motivational approach, e.g., in an effort to explain why certain contradictions and imagery emerge as central.

58. Cited in Deutscher, 77.

59. Freeland, 385.

60. For example, Lucien Goldmann's *The Hidden God: A Study of Tragic Vision in the Pensées of Pascal and the Tragedies of Racine*, trans. Philip Thody (London: Routledge and Kegan Paul, 1964). I raise these issues in my review of Deutscher's book in *Hypatia*, vol. 14, no. 3, Summer 1999, 157–162.

61. Jacques Derrida, *Of Grammatology*, trans. Gayatri Chakravorty Spivak (Baltimore: Johns Hopkins Press, 1976), 159, 158, cited in Deutscher, 86–87.

62. Irigaray, *An Ethics of Sexual Difference*, 5. Note that Irigaray's more recent work explicitly seeks to live up to the injunction for ethical and political intervention, through her discussion of civil codes and her argument for sexed civil rights. (See *Le temps de la difference: Pour une révolution pacifique* [1989] and *Je, tu, nous* [1990].)

63. Cynthia Freeland's article discusses these two approaches laid out in Michael Frede's paper "The History of Philosophy as a Discipline" (1988). He names the first approach as exegetical history of philosophy and the second approach as doxography. (Freeland, 371ff.).

64. Freeland, 403.

65. Susan James interviews Genevieve Lloyd and Moira Gatens, *Hypatia*, vol. 15, no. 2, Spring 2000, 45.

66. Deutscher, "A Matter of Affect, Passion and Heart," 15.

67. Deutscher, 10.

CHAPTER TWO

~

Feminist Epistemologies

What counts as knowledge and where knowledge counts?

During the spring semester of my first year of graduate school at Yale University, I was given the task of writing a long paper on Plato. I discovered to my surprise that my brain had turned into wood. I was simply unable to *think* about how to start the paper. In addition to the obvious psychological manifestation of anxiety, there were other factors that worked to freeze me intellectually. I expected that as a graduate student in philosophy I could produce objective thoughts about Plato that were untainted by my own personal interests and concerns. And I expected these thoughts to emerge like perfect pearls from my brow, as Athena herself had emerged full-blown from Zeus's brow. Panic somehow got me through the ordeal, but the crisis became a productive occasion to arrange a writing tutorial for the following year with my future dissertation advisor. During the next autumn, having immersed myself in Nietzsche's *Genealogy of Morals*, I began to explore how certain myths about philosophy had contributed to my mental paralysis: myths about objectivity as detached from individuals' desires, interests, wills, or perspectives. Nietzsche's own perspectivism is articulated in the third essay of the *Genealogy of Morals*:

> Let us, from now on, be on our guard against the hallowed philosophers' myth of a "pure, will-less, painless, timeless knower"; let us beware of the tentacles of such contradictory notions as "pure reason," "absolute

knowledge," "absolute intelligence." All these concepts presuppose an eye such as no living being can imagine, an eye required to have no direction, to abrogate its active and interpretative powers—precisely those powers that alone make of seeing, seeing *something*. All seeing is essentially perspective, and so is all knowing. The more emotions we allow to speak in a given matter, the more different eyes we can put on in order to view a given spectacle, the more complete will be our conception of it, the greater our 'objectivity.' But to eliminate the will, to suspend the emotions altogether, provided it could be done—surely this would be to castrate the intellect, would it not?[1]

It was precisely these myths—that philosophical reasoning produces truths that are pure, timeless, and absolute—that had contributed to my earlier crisis. For my own thinking was surely not purified of my own concerns, particularly of the fact that I was reading Plato as a woman and, hence, already haunted by the following troubling questions: Why does the body threaten to interfere with the discovery of truth? Why are women's bodies viewed as especially threatening? Nor was I oblivious of the self-punishing character of this myth, which Nietzsche characterized as part of the ascetic philosophical ideal. Writing my way through this crisis, I tried to reclaim myself instead of trying to think as an abstract intellectual entity. I used this existential crisis to thematize questions about knowledge and objectivity in my subsequent work on Kant: If knowledge is always situated, how does one understand the philosophical attempt to transcend situatedness? What conceptions of knowledge or objectivity could one offer as an alternative to the ideal of detached, disinterested, value-free objectivity—to what Donna Haraway calls the "god-trick" in science and philosophy? In facing my own situatedness, I began my first incursions into feminist philosophy. And it is the theme of situatedness that is still dominant in feminist discussions of knowledge and objectivity. As the Austrian philosopher Herta Nagl-Docekal writes, "Es gibt heute kein Zurück mere hinter die These von der Situiertheit der Forschung."[2] (There is today no turning back from the thesis of the situatedness of research.)

But before I discuss how feminist philosophy has contributed to discussions about knowledge and objectivity, let me clarify some common misconceptions about the field. First, feminist theorists do *not* argue that there is a special women's logic or that women biologically

[handwritten marginal notes at top of page, partially legible:]
"different" → doesn't ... women are ... but argue that ... that should ... information
... → doesn't eliminate "truth"

have access to ways of thinking that are foreclosed to men. Expressions like "women's ways of knowing" have been used,[3] but this phrase refers to the ways in which experiential differences between men and women, developing from psychological and social factors, shape different cognitive interests. This phrase underlines the view that knowledge is contextual and constructed, and that the dominant paradigms of learning are biased in favor of men's experiences. Hence, feminist epistemologists do not argue that cognitive differences are rooted in biological differences between the sexes. Nor do they argue that sexual difference provides a kind of transcendental foundation—beyond any given context—for grounding differences in cognitive styles that exist within specific contexts. But they do argue that the playing field in which human beings know and reflect on their knowledge is not an open one. It is a playing field that is figured by sexual differences, and by gendered and racial hierarchies. Hence, epistemology requires a self-reflexive critical practice that interrogates the function and effects of these differences and operations of power.

Second, feminist work with theories of knowledge and methodologies in the natural and social sciences do *not* signal a collapse of these fields, nor a rejection of terms like truth, objectivity, or rationality. On the contrary, as I hope to show in this book, feminists critically engage with these concepts to reconstruct them, not destroy them. And the reconstruction of terms like truth and objectivity takes account of the context of knowledge practices and norms, and the situatedness of the knower, without adopting a relativistic position.[4]

As the preceding chapter indicates, feminist work in the history of philosophy has largely been a critical discourse on concepts of reason, probing the unstable character of "male" and "female" in concepts of reason, and the way in which reason has been figured as detached from emotional and embodied life. In German-speaking countries, feminist theorists draw inspiration from Max Weber, Max Horkheimer, and Theodor Adorno to criticize the repressive features of instrumental rationality that support patriarchal domination. Although in this chapter I focus on theories of knowledge, echoes of the critical questions raised regarding concepts of rationality will be heard here as well. I will take up my discussion of ethics, or what philosophers since Kant have called practical reason, in the following chapter.

Work in feminist epistemology, together with work by black philosophers and marxist philosophers about the nature of knowledge, can be termed alternative epistemologies. Much of the feminist literature in this area veers away from questions that are central to mainstream analytic epistemology, e.g., about the existence of the external world, of other minds, and the reliability of perception and memory. Feminists have been less concerned with the question of how to prove the existence of other minds than with the question: why is the existence of other minds so problematic? Why do so many theories about knowledge presuppose an isolated knower, as if this knower did not have a body that was birthed and nourished by others, as if the knower had not learned a social language in which to express doubt? Feminist epistemologies are typically critical of the presuppositions of mainstream theories: (1) that the subject of knowledge is an individual who is essentially identical to and substitutable with other individuals; (2) that the object of knowledge is a natural object known by propositional knowledge, expressed in the form S-knows-that-p; (3) that objective knowledge is impartial and value free. Instead, feminists situate the knower as an embodied member of a community; they broaden the scope of knowledge to take knowledge of persons as at least as important as knowledge of natural objects, thereby acknowledging the role of feeling and doing in knowledge; and they emphasize that objectivity is not jeopardized but strengthened by the contextualization of the practices of knowledge and its norms of justification. Thus, feminists incorporate work on the history of knowledge practices into work on theories of knowledge. Instead of asking the skeptical questions of whether knowledge is possible at all or whether memory is reliable, those working with alternative epistemologies ask: Why have women been thought not to have knowledge? Why has memory failed in relation to the achievements of African civilization?[5]

Feminist epistemologies, like these other alternative epistemologies, can be understood as a contribution to social epistemology. Social epistemology begins from the basic insight that the social world is the only place from which one can make epistemological judgments. It investigates the social organization of knowledge, and the way in which granting epistemic authority has the effect of distributing power.[6] Whereas critics of feminist epistemology argue that nothing is offered by feminists to the more general project of social epistemology, it should be stressed that social epistemologists like Steve Fuller analyze the production and distribution and redistribution of knowledge without any mention of issues relating to gender or race. Rather, the nonfeminist approach presents an analysis of the social relations among knowledge producers that is fully sanitized of the factors that link social identity or power with epistemic authority. Thus, feminist epistemologists provide a necessary supplement to social epistemology. They acknowledge that a theory of knowledge must address questions about the nature of the social community, power, and desire, while at the same time they maintain with other social epistemologists a normative dimension that refuses to reduce knowledge to sociological observations. Elizabeth Potter and Linda Martín Alcoff, in their anthology *Feminist Epistemologies*, summarize questions that appear frequently in debates on this topic.

> Who is the subject of knowledge? How does the social position of the subject affect the production of knowledge? What is the impact upon knowledge and reason of the subject's sexed body? Is all knowledge expressible in propositional form? How can objectivity be maximized if we recognize that perspective cannot be eliminated? Are the perspectives of the oppressed epistemically privileged? How do social categories such as gender affect scientists' theoretical decisions? What is the role of the social sciences in the naturalization of epistemology? What is the connection between knowledge and politics?[7]

Recognizing that knowledge is a social enterprise has a number of implications. Since the knower is understood to be part of a community, one is prompted to ask: How do negotiations take place within these communities to solve disputes about knowledge? What theoretical approach is best suited to account for the collectivist character of knowledge? Linda Martín Alcoff argues that an approach based on coherentism, which views knowledge as a product of beliefs and practices that are immanent to social organizations and lived reality, is best suited to grasp the collectivist nature of knowledge processes. She contrasts her approach with foundationalism, which views truth as a relationship to an external realm beyond beliefs and practices and presumes that it is both possible and necessary to step outside our language practices and interpretations in order to have access to an extrahuman reality. Antifoundationalists argue that the foundationalists' belief in an extrahuman reality is one of the myths by which philosophy has elevated as ideal the notion of disinterested, impartial knowledge, attainable by isolated, substitutable individuals.

Acknowledging the social nature of knowledge brings to light questions about the values that guide knowing. Although the term "real" is often used as a contrast to the notion of perspective, both etymologically and historically the term "real" has implicitly acknowledged a particular perspective, i.e., one that was correlated with rank and privilege. (In premodern Europe, it was the prerogative of the papal inquisitor or of the king and his court to become the arbiter of truth.[8]) The Enlightenment did not eliminate the authorization of a particular perspective in accounts of truth, but it shifted this authorization to the new middle groups. In his book *The Social History of Truth*, Steven Shapin notes that in seventeenth-century England slaves, peasants, and any others who were beholden to others for their livelihood (including all women), were assumed to act in an agreeable matter out of necessity. Hence, it was thought that only with difficulty could lower-class people develop the virtue of truthfulness. The very rich and powerful were also considered unreliable, because of their interest in protecting the court and thwarting their enemies. "It was very widely understood in sixteenth- and seventeenth-century English society that the possession of great power and responsibility might compromise integrity, and that places of power were places where truth could thrive only with the greatest difficulty. . . . By contrast, the middle position might be accounted the place where scope for free action was greatest."[9] Hence, the concepts of reason and truth that were developed in the Enlightenment are not paragons of impartiality, but are structured by a particular kind of subjectivity.

Recognizing the social history of truth has encouraged feminist philosophers to deal explicitly with the relation between values and knowledge. Rejecting the myth of value-free knowledge does not imply that knowledge becomes reduced to values. This common objection presumes that there is no alternative to positivistic approaches to knowledge or science. Instead, feminist and other alternative epistemologies make possible a self-conscious debate about the nature of values that do guide the theories and practices of knowledge. For feminist philosophy, which has been inspired by feminism as a political movement, there is a conscious embrace of values that are democratic and emancipatory, rather than authoritarian and elitist. Moreover, feminist epistemologies, like other social epistemologies, make visible the social theories that are implicit in differing approaches to knowledge. And they criticize the social theory implicit in standard accounts of knowledge, which presumes that the knower is not only isolated from all others and substitutable with all others, but also is a white male knower in a Western capitalist country. Feminist epistemologists argue that knowledge *can* be improved. But improvement in knowledge is not primarily a question of individuals carrying out their analyses more exactly. Rather, improvement occurs by revising the paradigms of knowledge so that they more adequately address the perspectives of knowers who do not fit into these traditional presuppositions about the knower or the scientist. In particular, feminist work in epistemology seeks to address the implications of gender, race, and colonial relations in theories and practices of knowledge.[10]

Feminist philosophers raise questions of legitimacy: What paradigms and practices of knowledge are legitimated? What kinds of cognitive experiences are excluded? The Canadian philosopher Lorraine Code, in her groundbreaking article "Taking Subjectivity into Account," argues against the positivist conception of knowledge that has been dominant in the natural and social sciences.[11] For positivists, sensory observation under ideal observational conditions is the primary source of knowledge. Knowers are presumed to be neutral spectators who have no affective predispositions or value relations that infringe on their separation from the object of knowledge. Objects are viewed as passive and inert. Knowledge claims are presented in propositional sentences with the form S-knows-that-p, which can be verified by observation. Although each individual knower is independent of others, his cognitive efforts are in principle replicable by any other individual under the same observational conditions. Implicit in positivist epistemology is a sharp dichotomy between facts and values.

Since value statements are not verifiable by appeal to sensory data, they are viewed as meaningless. In this approach, scientific knowledge is treated as paradigmatic for knowledge in general. Karl Popper writes, "Epistemology I take to be the theory of *scientific knowledge*."[12] Moreover, a positivist approach to knowledge makes a sharp distinction between the context-of-discovery and the context-of-justification. Even though in fact information gathering may be contaminated by circumstances in everyday life, this contamination has no bearing on the principle of rational justification of knowledge. Positivists criticize the attempts to relate social or historical contexts to *theories* of knowledge as being guilty of the genetic fallacy, of reducing the justification of knowledge claims to the genesis of those claims. Although this description presents the positivist position in its starkest form, nonetheless it is these characteristics that have had a profound impact on methodologies of the human and social sciences and on everyday beliefs about the nature of knowledge.

Although my focus in this chapter is on feminist contributions to epistemology, philosophers identified with the traditions of phenomenology and existentialism have contributed compelling criticisms of objectivity, many of which have inspired feminist theorists. In Denmark one should note Søren Kierkegaard's major work *Afsluttende Uvidenskabelig Efterskrift* (*Concluding Unscientific Postscript*), especially his discussion of the subjective thinker.[13] More recently, K. E. Løgstrup has criticized positivist accounts for failing to account for the role of understanding, language, and theory in perception, and for failing to acknowledge that the surrounding world that human beings seek to know is a world made up not just of objects but also of persons and historical events.[14] My purpose here is not to privilege feminist accounts as unique in criticizing a positivist approach to knowledge. But I do seek to show how feminists draw out the consequences of these more general critiques to underline specifically the implications of sex, gender, and race for knowledge, themes that are not analyzed by these nonfeminist thinkers.

Even though positivists reject the view that there are any subjective components of knowledge (e.g., values, interests, and emotions), the positivist position is itself produced by "hidden subjectivities."[15] This approach to knowledge is put forward by professional philosophers, who are typically white men, but who nonetheless claim to provide a "view from nowhere." Feminist criticisms show that positivism is indeed a "view from somewhere," and this somewhere is only one possible option—and not the most productive one—for understanding the nature of knowledge.

The favored examples of positivists are simple objects or sensory posits—tables, chairs, patches of color. Since these are taken to be the most basic elements of experience, these examples purportedly ground philosophical analyses in everyday experiences. But this approach to daily experience is one that is based on a large degree of abstraction from context. I do not usually perceive the world as built up of simple objects like chairs, unless of course I am sitting on a chair as I am at this moment of writing. And then what is significant about the chair is not just its sheer existence as an object, but its comfort, design, and practicality. When I turn my attention to the chair I am sitting on in my office, I speculate about the university's failure to provide ergonomically adequate chairs for its employees and the economic reasons for this state of affairs. My attention is not directed to the chair as a collection of sensory data, but as an object for use. Even simple objects of experience are mediated by the subject's encounter with them. But positivists fail to take the subject into account; they present simple objects as artificially reduced and removed from a meaningful context of experience for the subject. Far from pointing to the building blocks of experience, the positivist orientation in knowledge abstracts from the complexity of real knowing that informs our knowledge of objects and of other persons. Implicit in Code's criticism of positivist-oriented epistemology is the question, what is the hidden subjective posture in positivism? The American biologist and science-studies theorist Evelyn Fox Keller uses psychoanalytic theory to give one answer to this question. She argues that the scientific norm of self-detached, impersonal objectivity is a consequence of the primacy of separateness in male ego development.[16] In her approach, aloofness from subjectivity is a mark of a certain kind of subject, i.e., the male subject who feels at home in a world of detachment. In her work on Barbara McClintock, winner of the Nobel Prize for her work on maize genetics, Keller suggests that scientific knowledge need not presuppose subjective aloofness. Rather, the imagination and creativity needed for scientific discoveries draw on the individual knower's use of holistic evidence and immersion in her or his field of inquiry.[17]

Moreover, feminist theorists argue against the widespread presupposition that knowledge is primarily about natural or scientific objects. They ask, why do we overlook knowledge of other persons as an important form of knowledge? As Seyla Benhabib notes in reference to social contract theorists, it is a strange world that philosophers presume in which "individuals are grown up before they have been born; in which boys are men before they have been children; a world where neither mother, nor sister, nor wife exists."[18] If other persons are crucial for the physical, emotional, linguistic, and social development of individuals, for the recognition that enables us to see ourselves as persons, why is epistemology not an inquiry into how we know other persons? These questions are crucial not only for our everyday use of the term "knowing" but also for methodological questions in the human and social sciences. Hence, feminist philosophers also explore what takes place in intimate spheres of daily life that are typically ignored by professional philosophers. They ask, How do we know people intimately, such as our partners or children? How do emotions carry out a large part of the work of this kind of knowledge? To know someone intimately requires that each person be open—at least from time to time—to the other. One knows each others' vulnerabilities, irreconcilable differences, and boundaries. Knowing another person is thus a reciprocal relation. One cannot be a knower without also being the person who is known. Knowledge in this sense is also an ethical relation and it places a demand to take responsibility for the other—a responsibility that is not always willingly accepted. This ethical relation is filled with an ambiguity of meanings and ambivalence of feeling, leading to continuously revised judgments based on both love and hatred. Intimate knowing is also a sensual relationship, between parent and child or between lovers. These affective, ethical, ambivalent, and sensual dimensions of knowledge reveal that knowing is an unending, changing process of a self that is absorbed in contradiction. Hence, the emotions, values, sensual relations, and social identity and location that configure individual subjectivity is the milieu in which knowing takes place. Without subjectivity in this sense, the claim to know another person would be a farce.

Although feminist epistemologists do not argue that knowing other persons should become the paradigm for all sorts of knowledge, they do argue that we should be reflective about the role of subjectivity in other forms of knowledge. Taking subjectivity into account leads to the question about reflexivity in both the natural and social sciences. Since cultures have agendas and make assumptions that individuals may not easily detect, these agendas and assumptions make their way into background assumptions and hypotheses that philosophers use. The American philosopher of science Sandra Harding argues that to maximize objectivity, one must critically examine these assumptions and beliefs on both the microscale of what takes place in a laboratory and on the macroscale of what takes place in a social order. In the case of the social sciences, Harding argues that reflexivity is only achieved when there is a reciprocity between the researcher and the persons studied, when research allows "the Other to gaze back 'shamelessly' at the self who had reserved for himself the right to gaze 'anonymously' at whoever he chooses."[19] Harding cites the example of two sociologists from Berkeley, California, who slowly began to understand that nothing could eliminate the colonial relations that existed between themselves, as white academics at a prestigious university, and the black informants in the community surrounding Berkeley whom they were studying. The only strategy for addressing this hierarchy is reflexivity. Reflexivity enables an understanding of the cultural particularity of the researcher, and of her or his theory and methods, and thus is a requirement for objectivity.

This emphasis on reflexivity is implicit in Code's approach as well, for she criticizes the view that S-knows-that-p can be an adequate description of knowledge. Code notes that it is not enough to know the content of the object P being studied; it is also necessary to know the nature and situation of S, who is studying it. Nor can one assume that biases that are evident in the context of discovery become corrected in the context of justification. "Evidence is *selected*, not found, and selection procedures are open to scrutiny. Nor can critical analysis stop there, for the funding and institutions that enable inquirers to pursue certain projects and not others explicitly legitimize the work. So the lines of accountability are long and interwoven; only a genealogy of their multiple strands can begin to unravel the issues," Code writes.[20] Both Code and Harding argue that taking subjectivity into account does not eliminate the possibility of knowledge but on the contrary is a condition for making objective knowledge possible.

Thus, feminists approach epistemology with the view that knowledge is more complex than philosophers typically have taken it to be. They ask, Why have professional philosophers in the Anglo-American tradition bracketed out this complexity and focused only on knowledge that can be expressed in the sentence "S-knows-that-p"? Vrinda Dalmiya and Linda Martín Alcoff argue that what one witnesses in epistemological debates is a kind of epistemic discrimination. By focusing only on "knowing that," philosophers have forgotten Aristotle's insight that "knowing how," or practical knowledge, is also a form of knowledge. Thus, professional philosophers have excluded many kinds of experiential knowledge from epistemological inquiries. In particular, the kind of knowledge once considered to be women's province, like midwives' knowledge of childbirth, becomes classified as old wives' tales and not a form of legitimate knowledge.[21]

To make room for a more egalitarian epistemology, it is necessary to expand the scope of knowledge to include experiential and practical knowledge that does not fit into the form of "knowing that." A glance at the history of midwifery shows how this form of knowledge became discredited in the nineteenth century. Prior to the nineteenth century, midwives were often respected members of the community because of their knowledge and skill in helping women with pregnancy, childbirth, and lactation. Midwives could turn the baby in the womb to avoid a breech presentation, perform abortions, and cure breast infections and had knowledge of herbal remedies that could hasten labor, lessen the pain of childbirth, and reduce the chance of miscarriages. Until the nineteenth century, many doctors recognized that midwives were just as successful in assisting women, if not more so, than trained physicians. And yet midwives' knowledge became discredited with the consolidation of male-dominated medical institutions and technological developments. Dalmiya and Alcoff argue that this development can be understood as "a triumph of propositional knowledge over practical knowledge."[22] The history of how midwives' knowledge became discredited is just one example of how the narrative of progress in knowledge has favored an intellectualist epistemological model while excluding the more experientially based form of practical knowledge.

The skeptical response to this proposal is to argue that practical knowledge can never be a question of truth. If there is no truth, then there is no way of evaluating the worth or worthlessness of particular claims for knowledge. One can respond to this objection by pointing out that there is a different logic in practical knowledge than there is in propositional knowledge. Knowledge in this sense is a matter of degree, not an all or nothing affair. But one does not forfeit normative judgments about the quality of experiential knowledge. People are better or worse at doing things like driving cars, baking bread, and rearing children. People can get better at these tasks through experience. And experience creates a self-awareness of one's abilities. The woman who is a first-time mother of a two-week-old infant and the same woman nine months later have different degrees of knowledge. Immediately after childbirth, a woman may feel unsure when confronted by the unprecedented and constant demands of caring for an infant. Nine months later, her experiential knowledge has increased dramatically. The change is not merely one of improved techniques, or reduced demands, though these occur as well. It is a change in her knowledge of her child—an understanding of what the child's needs are, how to recognize them, and how to gauge their urgency—as well as a confidence that she can meet the child's needs. Knowledge in this context is a temporal, intersubjective process. Knowledge should not be taken only in this experiential sense, but it is crucial to expand the scope of knowledge explored by philosophers to include these cognitive experiences.[23] If one does not want to discriminate against certain kinds of knowing and certain kinds of knowers, then one must give up the philosophical expectation of having a unitary norm for all kinds of truths and explore how knowledge is situated and perspectival.

One might meet the following objection, typically raised in debates about social constructivism: whereas human social realities are constituted through historical and linguistic practices, natural realities have a different ontological nature and a different kind of truth claim. Hence, the subjective experience of the knower plays no role in the natural sciences.[24] Feminist theorists like Code, Harding, Alcoff, and Donna Haraway all argue for some form of constructivism in the natural as well as social sciences, though they are wary of a radical constructivism that loses a commitment to giving an account of the "real world." As Haraway poses the problem: "So, I think my problem and 'our' problem is how to have *simultaneously* an account of radical historical contingency for all knowledge claims and knowing subjects, a critical practice for recognizing our 'semiotic technologies' for making meanings, *and* a nonnonsense commitment to faithful accounts of a 'real' world."[25]

Haraway's work on the history of science, particularly the studies of primates, shows that the content of knowledge of the nonhuman world is also value laden. For example, research carried out by Clarence Ray Carpenter on rhesus monkeys in the late 1930s was based on a number of assumptions linking sex and dominance. He performed an experiment on a group of rhesus monkeys that consisted in removing the dominant three males over a three-week period and then restoring them to the group. Carpenter concluded that when the dominant males were removed, social order was seriously disrupted, there was an increase in intragroup conflicts, and the group lost its favorable position relative to other groups. His study established a dominance hierarchy among the males as the source of social order, reaching conclusions similar to those in studies of the authoritarian personality and competitive aggressiveness among human beings conducted during the same period. But interestingly, Carpenter did not use as a control for his experiment the removal of any other than the dominant males. Haraway shows by contrast that revisionist work in primatology stresses principles of organization that do not depend on dominance hierarchies. Revisionists examine dominance structures, but do not treat them as the causal explanation for the functioning of the group. Instead, they stress the role of matrifocal groups and long-term social cooperation, with flexible processes rather than rigid structures.[26]

Thus, feminist work in epistemology has criticized approaches that oversimplify the event of knowledge, which overlook its subjective and intersubjective components, which devalue the role of experience, and that disregard the role of values and power at work in this collective enterprise. At the same time, feminist theorists have not rejected the traditional goal of gaining objective knowledge. Yet their characterization of objectivity differs from that commonly found in the corridors of philosophy institutes. Haraway's discussion of situated knowledge is one of the most rhetorically powerful visions of what is involved in re-working objectivity. The dilemma for Haraway is to negotiate the tension between (1) recognizing that all knowledge is partial and local and that one must abandon any dreams of transcendence, omnipotence, or immortality and (2) maintaining a commitment to giving an account of the "real" world that is translatable among different communities. To bridge what seem like contradictory positions, i.e., the position of radical constructivism and of critical empiricism, Haraway reintroduces the metaphor of vision for knowing that has been in disrepute among feminists because of its historical role in detaching perception from embodied existence. She proposes to think of vision as embodied; hence, vision is as varied as the bodies that see. Haraway contrasts the vision of dogs, which have few retinal cells for color vision, with the compound eyes of an insect and with the camera eye that provides to the readers of *National Geographic* detailed pictures of an embryo in the womb or of a man on the moon. Seeing, whether organic or mechanical, is an active perceptual process that gives a detailed, but always partial, way of organizing worlds. She writes, "Understanding how these visual systems work, technically, socially, and psychically ought to be a way of embodying feminist objectivity."[27]

In emphasizing that all knowing is situated, one avoids both the god-trick of totalization—of transcending any particular location—and the god-trick of relativism—of being nowhere while claiming to be everywhere equally. One arrives instead at a conception of objectivity as critical, partial, and locatable. Critical positioning, in Haraway's approach, is not a question of *being* a particular kind of identity. She rejects identity approaches, which often end up in essentializing positions, such as that of the "Third World Woman." Rather, critical positioning is a strategy for taking responsibility for one's position, and thus it implies that ethics and politics are decisive in the struggle over what counts as rational knowledge. In Haraway's vision, not only is seeing–knowing an active process, but the objects one sees—whether human or natural—are also understood to be active agents, not passive objects for discovery and manipulation. Thus, knowledge of the 'real world' is a reciprocal relation, a "power-charged social relation of 'conversation.'"

Haraway's vision of situated knowledge has a number of advantages. In conceptualizing the active character of both subjects and objects of knowledge, her approach shows that knowledge production is an on-going process of creation, not a static result. By exploring the technical, social, and psychical procedures by which knowledge is attained, it shows that epistemology is simultaneously a critical inquiry into its own conditions of production. Nonetheless, Haraway does not answer the objections typically raised by epistemologists: How can one evaluate competing claims to knowledge? How does thinking of knowledge in terms of embodied and positioned vision give us tools for arguing that some claims to knowledge are less partial than others or that partial claims to knowledge are related to each other in definable ways? One needs to extend Haraway's conception of situated knowledge to include an analysis of how different positions from which knowledge is produced are related to each other. But a relational analysis of knowledge production will still be a view from somewhere. Thus, it will not satisfy critics who seek to separate an analysis of the production of knowledge from procedures of epistemological justification. Nor will it satisfy the critics of relativism who ask, How can one avoid the claim that any view is equally valid? The question of how to justify particular perspectives is of especial concern in relation to moral and political questions; e.g., how is one to know whether abortion is killing or not? But as Haraway and other feminist theorists note, many disputes about knowledge are ultimately decided by ethical and political commitments. Hence, alternative epistemologists are explicit about their open and democratic conception of knowledge, and they stress that debates about values and power need to be an intrinsic element in theories of knowledge.

Thus, the critical discussion by feminist epistemologists focuses on the failure by mainstream epistemologists to take subjectivity and situatedness explicitly into account, with consequent ideological distortions. The constructive attempts to revamp objectivity take as their starting point a self-conscious recognition of the social nature of the subject of knowledge. Feminist epistemologists today do *not* invert the dualisms of Western culture—rational/irrational, subject/object, culture/nature, male/female—to revalorize the second term in each pair. Rather, feminists show how existing configurations of power and reason have constructed these polarities, and they seek to develop accounts of knowledge that subvert these dualistic structures.

Typically, feminist discussions of objectivity work their way through the following positions: feminist empiricism, feminist standpoint theory, and postmodernism. My discussion of feminist empiricism and feminist standpoint theory will focus on their implications for general questions of epistemology rather than on specific debates in philosophy of science. Furthermore, I will not focus on postmodernism per se in the subsequent discussion. Many insights associated with the loose term "postmodernism" do inform my presentation of feminist epistemologies: the role of language and interpretation in constituting knowledge and knowers, the rejection of foundationalism, the emphasis on dissolving dualisms. And the work of the French philosopher Michel Foucault has been crucially important for feminist theorists. His account of the discursive construction of subjectivity, his focus on the history of truth and the emancipatory possibilities of carrying out a genealogy of truth, and his analysis of knowledge as consisting of a network of many different practices and of the interrelations between knowledge and power make a vital contribution to rethinking epistemology.[28] Yet many thinkers identified with postmodernism reject an explicitly epistemological project and do not develop the reconstructive possibilities inherent in their critiques.[29] Hence, in the final section I will focus on the coherentist account of knowledge developed by Linda Martín Alcoff, who seeks to develop an account of knowledge that is cognizant of postmodernist debates. Alcoff argues for an account of knowing that is collectivist, rather than individualist, that can account for the disparate elements involved in theory choice, and that nonetheless retains an account of truth.

Feminist empiricists take as their starting point the view that knowledge is based on empirical evidence; hence, "nature" remains one of the primary constraints on knowledge. They maintain the empiricist approach to evidence while challenging two central presuppositions of empiricism, as it has been developed by writers like Locke, Berkeley, Hume, or the logical empiricists. Feminist empiricists break away from epistemological individualism, and they challenge the hard boundary between knowledge and values usually associated with empiricism.[30] Instead, they focus on the social nature of the subject of knowledge. The American philosopher Helen Longino argues for cognitive democracy, based on the view that knowledge is constructed by

an interactive dialogic community. In her view, knowledge is the out-
come of public, critical dialogue within communities that (a) have the
ability to change their beliefs and theories over time and (b) recognize
equal cognitive authority for differing perspectives and do not align
cognitive authority with political or economic power. Her proposal
breaks away from the belief in the possibility or desirability of universal consensus or absolute truth. She considers objectivity to be socially
constituted, built on ongoing interactions with natural and social en-
vironments, and open to correction or transformation.[31]

A stronger account of the social nature of the subject of knowledge
is put forth by the feminist empiricist Lynn Hankinson Nelson, who argues that the agents of knowledge are not individuals at all, but "epistemic communities." Her account of epistemic communities underlies
her critique of individualism: none of us knows what no one else could
know. The conditions for individuals to have knowledge include their
being members of sociolinguistic communities, having access to public
conceptual schemes that shape experience into something coherent,
and sharing assumptions, beliefs, and theories that are historically relative.[32] Thus, communities are epistemologically prior to the knowing
that individuals do. Nelson makes the following claims for feminist empiricism: (1) Empirical studies of the history, social relations, and practices of communities are part of the scope of epistemology and
(2) epistemology, as the study of how we build knowledge and the evidence we have for doing so, is a fully empirical project. Hence, she
follows W. V. Quine in naturalizing epistemology. In this account, epistemology cannot provide a justification for our knowledge claims.
Rather, it begins with the assumption that we do in fact know and pro-
ceeds to examine how we make sense of experience.

Feminist empiricism is often viewed as a conservative discourse by
nonempiricist feminists, because it allegedly sees the sexism in scientific knowledge as a result of letting prejudice interfere with
scientific inquiry. According to Sandra Harding, feminist empiricists
believe that you can "add woman and stir," and they fail to take a
more radical stance toward revising the concept of objectivity. But
feminist empiricists do problematize empiricism's individualistic assumptions and its split between knowledge and values. Nonetheless,
feminist empiricists do not resolve the fundamental issues of social

epistemology, namely, the questions of cognitive authority and normativity.

Longino's vision of cognitive democracy is based on an epistemological pluralism that presumes an equality of intellectual authority. However, in contestations about knowledge, one partner to the debate typically refuses to recognize opponents' equal intellectual authority. For example, those who are hostile to feminist philosophy view themselves as unbiased spokespersons for knowledge, while feminist philosophers are disqualified from equal standing. Longino's conception of an interactive dialogic community has the same weakness as other forms of pluralism: it neglects to analyze the effects of existing power structures. By overlooking the fact that not all positions are granted equal cognitive authority, pluralism cedes the question of normativity to those already authorized institutionally to define knowledge. Since communities are often averse to dissent and reluctant to revise their beliefs and theories, cognitive norms that affect the concrete practices of job appointments and research funding will be articulated by established authorities within a community.

Nelson takes an empirical study of communities' practices as vital for epistemology; hence, her account provides a better position from which to study the established hierarchies that channel the production of knowledge. Insofar as communities are actually subject to criticism by other communities or subcommunities, knowledge reflects the challenges posed by these critical subcommunities. However, this empirical account is unable to address the role of normativity in epistemology. In this account, naturalized epistemology cannot provide a justification for knowledge, yet it is not merely descriptive. Rather, epistemology provides a reconstruction of experience and knowledge by "recasting the experiences of those involved so as to make the most overall sense."[33] Thus, epistemology evaluates knowledge claims and the processes by which those claims are generated. Epistemology, in Nelson's approach, includes the study of historical patterns in the construction of de facto norms, but it provides no role for the justification of cognitive norms.

Whereas feminist empiricists analyze the social character of the agents of knowledge and the role of particular practices and values in generating knowledge, they do not offer a social theory about the nature of this collectivity. Another prominent strand in feminist epistemology, standpoint theory, *is* committed to a particular theory about the nature of collectivities in which knowledge is produced. Nancy Hartsock's article "The Feminist Standpoint: Developing the Ground for a Specifically Feminist Historical Materialism" was groundbreaking in developing a sophisticated feminist theoretical framework inspired by a marxist conception of standpoint. Hartsock discusses the epistemological underpinnings of Karl Marx's concept of historical materialism to analyze the epistemological implications of the sexual division of labor. The theory of the standpoint of the proletariat suggested by Marx and subsequently developed by Georg Lukács in *History and Class Consciousness*, claims that the vantage of the oppressed class is privileged in revealing the truth of the social order. Whereas those identified with ruling class interests articulate their particular class interests in their theoretical productions, those who are oppressed by the class structure are able to articulate a true vision of social relations. Hartsock draws out the implications of standpoint theory. (1) Material life structures and sets limits to the understanding of the social order. (2) The vision available to those in the dominant position in class relations will be partial and perverse. (3) The vision of the oppressed group is not immediate but mediated. It is an achievement that is attained by seeing beneath the surface of social relations in which the oppressed are forced to participate. (4) Their vision emerges from the struggle to change existing social relations; hence, it is an engaged and emancipatory vision that seeks the liberation of all human beings.[34]

With this theoretical framework, Hartsock develops the notion of the standpoint of women in the sexual division of labor in capitalist societies, by which she seeks to "lay aside the important differences among women across race and class boundaries and instead search for central commonalities." The sexual division of labor points to women's activity in reproduction. Not only do they reproduce the lives of existing laborers through their household labor but they also reproduce the next generation of workers through their role as mothers and nurturers. From the point of view of marxist and socialist feminists, the analysis of sensuous activity carried out by Marx should be extended beyond the domain of production to include the sensuous activity involved in sustaining life itself.[35] In this approach, the sexual division of labor is viewed as structuring both men's and women's vision. Men's perspective reflects their experience of abstract masculinity, of being removed from the work of renewing life; hence, it is partial. Women's perspective is relationally defined and results from their work in transforming both physical objects and human beings. Hence, women's standpoint provides a framework that exposes the limits of the male standpoint and provides a basis for moving beyond these relations.[36]

This approach has implications for epistemology. (1) The subject of knowledge is social and needs to be understood through an analysis of class and sexual relations. (2) Social positions and perspectives are coupled, and there is no value-neutral perspective. (3) Perspectives are not merely different but one perspective—that of the oppressed—is privileged in providing objectivity. (4) This privileged perspective has emancipatory implications for all members of society. These arguments grew out of the feminist revision of marxist and socialist theories in the 1970s and 1980s, and they remained powerful theoretical tools during these years.

With the increased influence of poststructuralist theory, many of these assumptions of standpoint theory have been called into question. The active debate about racism and heterosexism within the women's movement raised the question of whether one can point to central commonalities among women, and whether constituting women along these commonalities constructs some individuals as women and excludes others. Furthermore, the notion of epistemic privilege has been transformed in varying ways. For lesbian feminists like Gayle Rubin and Pat Califia, epistemic privilege measures intensity in the degree of transgression, as in sadomasochistic sexual practices. Other writers use epistemic privilege to chart the multiplication of oppressive systems (sex, class, race, heterosexism). But in all these variants, writers have assumed a single center from which oppression stems. The Israeli-American feminist Bat-Ami Bar On argues that it is important to understand the multiple centers of oppression, refute the idealization of marginalization, and recognize that authorizing one marginalized position may be yet another exclusionary practice.[37] Moreover, standpoint epistemology is committed to some Enlightenment notions that are problematic for many feminists inspired by Foucault's work—e.g., the assumption that there is a comprehensive truth, instead of viewing this claim as another effect of power; the assumption that there is a unitary system of power, as opposed to multiple strategies of power; and the assumption that it is possible to be fully emancipated from relations of power.

Therefore, many feminist theorists accept the first two claims of standpoint theory, regarding the relation between social position and perspective, and qualify the fourth claim, arguing that epistemological theories should be democratic and contribute to emancipation. But they reject the third claim about the existence of a privileged perspective. Hence, the term "situated knowledge" that is prevalent in contemporary feminist discourse expresses in part the materialist turn in epistemology opened up by marxist theory. Nonetheless, situated knowledge implies a reworking of concepts of power and subjectivity.

Sandra Harding has attempted to revise standpoint epistemology in light of objections raised by poststructuralist theorists. She acknowledges the multiple and fragmented nature of subjectivity and the splits and conflicts among women that belie the view of a uniform women's experience. Moreover, Harding does not consider the domination of women as independent of domination based on race, class, or colonial relations. She develops a concept of strong objectivity that is historically and culturally relative, but not epistemologically relative. In her view, knowledge is always situated—hence, partial—but there are reasonable standards by which one can choose epistemological judgments that are less partial and less distorted than others. Thus, one can maintain the insight of standpoint theory that epistemological questions ought to begin with the experience of marginalized lives, while recognizing that this strategy is not itself a solution to epistemological problems. In both the natural and social sciences, this starting point must be linked with what Harding calls strong reflexivity, by which the researcher puts herself or himself on the same critical plane as the objects of research. Only then will it be possible to examine critically how culturewide beliefs function in both the context of discovery and the context of justification. In motivating epistemological inquiries by the experience of marginalization, Harding shifts the concept of standpoint beyond women's lives to include the effects of racism and colonialism in science.[38] However, Harding's concept of strong objectivity is not in fact an argument for a new methodology; it is rather a strategy for developing reflexivity in theory and for making *feminist* uses of existing methodologies. For example, she writes that "this directive leaves open to be determined within each discipline or research area what a researcher must do to start thought from women's lives or the lives of people in other marginalized groups."[39] And elsewhere she writes, "My point here is to argue against the idea of a distinctive feminist method of research."[40] The concept of reflexivity, which has been debated within the social sciences, is not what is new in her conception of strong objectivity; nor does she reconceptualize method. Rather, the newness of a feminist conception of strong objectivity results from linking existing research methods with a feminist commitment to provide knowledge *for* women and marginalized people. Harding argues that the politics of feminism enables the production of a strong form of objectivity, which is not merely one partial perspective among many. Although Harding presumes that marginalization by means of gender, class, race, and colonialism generates standpoints for achieving maximal objectivity, she does not clarify the relations among these standpoints. Sometimes she unifies these standpoints by focusing on one feature that they all share, that is, the gender components in the different systems. Sometimes Harding's unifying gesture lies in assuming a parallel structure between the center and different kinds of marginalization.

The black American theorist Patricia Hill Collins, in *Black Feminist Thought*, borrows the language of standpoint epistemology to validate the subjugated knowledge of black women. She argues that a self-defined Afrocentric feminist standpoint authorizes the voice of black women and enables empowerment and resistance. Collins argues that black societies in Africa, the Caribbean, South America, and North America share Afrocentric values that permeate family structures, religious institutions, culture, and community life. These societies reflect core African values that existed before the modern history of racial oppression. Moreover, as a result of colonialism, slavery, and apartheid, black people share a "common experience of oppression."[41] This combination of Afrocentric values and the experience of racial oppression has created a distinctively Afrocentric epistemology that has points of contact with feminist standpoint theories. Collins suggests that black women have a both–and conceptual orientation, because they are simultaneously a member of a group and yet stand apart from it. In certain respects black women resemble black men; in other respects, they resemble white women; and in other respects, they stand apart from both groups. The complexity of their position vis à vis other groups constitutes what Bonnie Thornton Dill has called the "dialectics of Black womanhood."[42]

In arguing for this both–and conceptual orientation, Collins explicitly distances herself from an add-on analysis of oppression, which adds the oppression of race and class to that of gender, and postulates that groups subject to all three forms of oppression have the most complete knowledge. An add-on approach bears the traces of a quantitative analysis of oppression, and it maintains the assumption that there is a single standpoint from which absolute truth can be attained. Collins argues instead that domination should be understood as a matrix of interlocking systems of oppression based on race, class, and gender.

Thus, Collins moves away from feminist standpoint theory in two ways. (1) She rejects the claim that gender provides a central commonality that race and class do not. All people participate in systems of racial oppression, though white people have the privilege of taking these systems for granted and thus rendering them invisible. Moreover, race cannot be separated from gender, as though sometimes a person is black and sometimes she is female. Thus, although Collins uses the language of standpoint, she moves away from a unifocal theory of domination. (2) Collins also explicitly rejects the notion that any standpoint provides maximal objectivity.

> A Black women's standpoint is only one angle of vision. Thus, Black feminist thought represents a partial perspective. The overarching matrix of domination houses multiple groups, each with varying experiences with penalty and privilege that produce corresponding partial perspectives, situated knowledges. . . . No one group possesses the theory or methodology that allows it to discover the absolute "truth" or, worse yet, proclaim its theories and methodologies as the universal norm evaluating other groups' experiences.[43]

Thus, Collins is committed to the notion that every standpoint is partial, and thus uses "standpoint" interchangeably with "situated knowledge." Although she does not elaborate a theory to discuss the relation between different standpoints, she does suggest a direction in which such a theory might be developed. The standpoints of different groups must be brought into dialogue with each other, and the ideas that are validated by "African-American women, African-American men, Latina lesbians, Asian-American women, Puerto Rican men, and other groups with distinctive standpoints . . . become the most 'objective' truths." In other words, Collins proposes a dialogic model of knowledge—itself immanent in an Afrocentric perspective—to find points of connection and resonance between different situations and standpoints. Nonetheless, like other standpoint theorists, Collins does tend to valorize the positive effects of oppression in generating resistance and transformative practice. In this sense, feminist standpoint theorists distort marxist theory, which takes seriously the ideological dimension of oppression, and they fail to consider the damage to personal character that occurs through oppression and violence.[44]

Typically, a presentation of feminist epistemologies moves through feminist empiricism, to feminist standpoint theory, to poststructuralism, which is frequently dismissed for its nihilism with regard to epistemology. Critics of poststructuralism accuse it of maintaining the position that knowledge is only an effect of power strategies. Since poststructuralism acknowledges only truths that are historically and culturally specific, they are presumed to reject the normative component of knowledge that has been the concern of epistemologists. However, philosophers like Sandra Harding and Linda Martín Alcoff do incorporate poststructuralist insights regarding the relation between discourse, power, and knowledge and the decentering of the subject into their epistemological endeavors. In her book *Real Knowing*, Alcoff has incorporated these insights within a full-fledged epistemological project, which she dubs a "robust coherentist epistemology."[45]

Alcoff emphasizes the situated nature of knowledge, but rejects the claim of standpoint epistemologists that there is a privileged perspective from which knowledge is maximized. She thereby acknowledges the historical realities of social and cognitive hierarchies. However, the originality of Alcoff's work lies in her argument that situated knowledge maintains a normative dimension and is not reduced to social or political categories.

Alcoff argues that it is necessary to maintain a notion of truth that makes sense of the intuition that truth is what really happened, without positing truth as correspondence to a mind-independent reality. Truth must be understood as indexed to a specific constellation of elements, which include theories, discourses, historical, spatiotemporal, and social locations. Since truth can be understood only in relation to these specifics, it is plural and changeable. It is an epistemological virtue to have a more extensive constellation of elements by which truth is analyzed, based on a fuller experience. The more one acknowledges the complexity of context, the more one works through contradictions, the closer one gets to a robust concept of coherence, which Alcoff uses as a limit notion toward which all knowledge seeking strives. This approach maintains a conception of truth as referring to, intervening in, and representing the whole of lived reality—the realities of birth and death and suffering and physical climactic changes—thus, it moves beyond a strict constructionist conception of reality. Moreover, this conception maintains the historically relative nature of truth, without reducing it to irrationality, subjectivism, or ideology.

Alcoff's distinctive contribution is to work through the normative component of epistemology in light of a conception of truth as always indexed to specific historical constellations. Her emphasis on specificity is in part inspired by Foucault's account of power/knowledge. For Foucault, knowledge is not determined by or subordinated to power, as his critics claim. Rather, Foucault regards truth as a thing of this world that comes into play only in practices and the interpretation of these practices. The dyadic concept of power/knowledge, which insists that knowledge can never leave aside relationships to the strategies and effects of power, serves to complicate and make more plausible the analysis of knowledge. Foucault's account of local knowledge also supports the notion of situated knowledge. Local, subjugated knowledges—e.g., that one finds among nurses who struggle in medical bureaucracies or among homosexuals who struggle against prejudice in their workplace and daily lives—do not seek to be global, hegemonic discourses; hence, they do not require violence, distortion, and omission to maintain themselves.[46]

Alcoff argues that Foucault's concept of power/knowledge does not undermine the possibility of normative judgments. One can make judgments by taking into account the complex contexts in which they are made. Theories can be evaluated as true or false at a particular time, given the current constellation of elements and the adequacy of the theory in accounting for this constellation. Implicitly, she abandons any claim to finding truths that are absolute or context independent. In this she also finds support in the work of Hans Georg Gadamer, who argues against an ahistorical, decontextualized methodology. Gadamer can also be viewed as a coherence theorist, who regards truth as consisting in the most comprehensively coherent interpretation. For Gadamer, like Foucault, truth is indexed to specific constellations of elements, though he provides few resources to understand what the specific indexical elements are.[47]

Alcoff charts out an important line of inquiry by which epistemological norms are understood to be relational—always in relation to particular contexts—and qualitative—taking account of the "nature, quality and comprehensiveness of the representation."[48] This notion of truth serves as a limit concept, a goal to strive for that is never absolutely attainable, rather than as a set of procedures or principles that can ensure us of truth. Thus, Alcoff expands epistemological frameworks without abandoning an epistemological project as such. She emphasizes the material parameters of human and natural existence that are beyond human control and, thus, links truth to a notion of lived reality that is not strictly a constructionist one. Alcoff develops an ontology of immanent realism that refers to the world of our bodies, our experiences, our theories of social hierarchies and relations, and our interpretive and linguistic construction of these realities without losing the notion of human limit in relation to these realities.

The Australian philosopher Elizabeth Grosz writes of the "sexualization of knowledges." With this phrase, she extends Nietzsche's insight into the cognitive significance of corporality and positionality, to consider explicitly the meaning and effects of sexual difference for knowledge.[49] Grosz's statement is rhetorically provocative, but she articulates a position held by many feminist philosophers. The construction of reason in the history of philosophy has typically excluded women and qualities associated with the feminine; many features of contemporary epistemology maintain the link between knowledge and the historically masculine attempt to escape embodiment.

Debates about feminist epistemologies face the question of the future: Will sexual difference continue to be a horizon for future discussions of rationality and knowledge? On the one side, those inspired by the French philosopher and psychoanalyst Luce Irigaray argue that sexual difference will continue to be the horizon on which to think of rationality, as well as ethics. Irigaray argues that Western rationality is linked to symbolic interpretations of the male and female body. Western rationality takes the symbolism of the phallus as primary and with it the principles of identity, noncontradiction, and binarism. These principles are based on the belief in the necessity of stable forms and in the supremacy of solids over fluids. The feminine, which Irigaray links to the symbolism of the "two lips" of the female body that are "neither one nor two" and, hence, with the challenge to individuation, thereby has been suppressed.[50] Irigaray does not propose to work out a logic of the feminine that parallels and counters existing structures of rationality. Rather, she takes her task to be that "of jamming the theoretical machinery itself, of suspending its pretension to the production of a truth and of a meaning that are excessively univocal."[51] Her strategy of disruption can create the condition necessary for the advent of woman as subject of philosophy, for recognizing woman, the Other of culture. Thus the conceptualization of rationality will always be inseparable from the conceptualization of male and female.

Other feminist theorists do not take sexual difference as the horizon for all future accounts of knowledge. Some, like Grosz and the Italian-Australian philosopher Rosi Braidotti, find inspiration in the work of Gilles Deleuze, who suggests that philosophy must be inventive, must engage with concepts that create new events, questions, and possibilities. Instead of just focusing on how things have been in the past—on memory and history—Grosz argues that we need to think a radical openness to the future. But Braidotti points to the ambivalent consequences for feminist theory of Deleuze's approach. On the one hand, Deleuze adopts the figure of "becoming woman" as the figure for renewal for culture, since woman is the privileged figure of otherness in Western culture. On the other hand, his notion of "becoming-woman" does not refer to the experience of empirical women, but to a general process of becoming. Deleuze's philosophy leads away from thinking within a horizon of sexual difference, and toward a notion that differences will proliferate into a multiplicity of sexed subjectivities. This has the positive benefit of guarding against taking sexual difference as a foundation for all future thought. But it has the negative effect of overlooking how sexual dissymmetry continues to structure the present, and of overlooking the role of time in struggling against this dissymmetry. Braidotti summarizes the implications of Deleuze for feminism as follows:

> In the short term Deleuze's radical reconceptualization erodes the foundations of a specific feminist epistemology and of a theory of feminine subjectivity insofar as it rejects the masculine/feminine dichotomy altogether. In the longer run, however, the radically projective concept of the intensive Deleuzean subject opens the door to possible configurations of a variety of subject-positions that are postmetaphysics of gender or beyond sexual difference.[52]

Situated knowledge implies that the material and symbolic horizon of knowledge in the present includes sexual difference, as well as racial and ethnic differences. The relative positions of sexual, racial, and ethnic differences depend on the specific context in which knowledge occurs and to which it is indexed. Marxist theorists approach the future through the contradictions of the present, and from this point of view, it is hard to ignore the existence of sexual difference as an inheritance in the future. Yet the future is also radically undecidable, and feminists are cautious about limiting the horizon of knowledge to what is already given.

Thus, the politics of knowledge needs to be thought in reference to both the present and the future. When speaking of the present, feminists challenge the dominant politics of knowledge to transform the subject of knowledge so as to include women as knowers and to take subjectivity into account. Feminists also challenge prevailing knowledge–power relations to account for the complex contexts in which living beings or things become objects of knowledge. In reference to the future, to which all action is oriented, feminist politics of knowledge includes an explicit emphasis on democratic and emancipatory values that will create more open and democratic knowledge in the future. On the epistemological level, the emphasis on a democratic politics of knowledge leads to a kind of perspectivism that is related to what one could call a pluralistic universalism that can grasp the complexity of social knowledge and different interpretations.[53] On the political level, it leads to pressure for institutional changes to recruit a diverse population among university students, teachers, and researchers that can open up knowledge and work toward creating more democratic institutions of learning than we have at present.

Notes

1. Friedrich Nietzsche, *The Birth of Tragedy and the Genealogy of Morals*, trans. Francis Golffing (New York: Doubleday, 1956), 255–56.

2. Herta Nagl-Docekal, *Feministische Philosophie* (Frankfurt am Main: Fischer Taschenbuch Verlag, 1999), 133. My translation.

3. For example, see Mary Field Belenky et al., *Women's Ways of Knowing* (New York: Basic Books, 1986), which builds on psychological and pedagogical theories of gender differences in learning.

4. Relativism is viewed as anathema by most philosophers, and feminist philosophers have been no less concerned to avoid it. Feminists want to be able to argue that discrimination against women or blacks or non-Danish immigrants is wrong and not just their idiosyncratic opinion. The philosophical question discussed below is how a contextualist approach to knowledge maintains a normative dimension.

5. Charles W. Mills, "Alternative Epistemologies," in *Epistemology: The Big Questions*, ed. Linda Martín Alcoff (Malden and Oxford: Blackwell, 1998), 392–93.

6. Steven Fuller, *Social Epistemology* (Bloomington and Indianapolis: University of Indiana Press, 1988), 3–12.

7. Elizabeth Potter and Linda Martín Alcoff, *Feminist Epistemologies* (New York: Routledge, 1993), 13.

8. Potter and Alcoff, *Feminist Epistemologies*, 201.

9. Steven Shapin, *Social History of Truth* (Chicago: University of Chicago Press, 1994), 100–1. Cited in Alcoff, 202.

10. As an example of the close connection between politics and theories of knowledge, see Sandra Harding, *Is Science Multicultural? Postcolonialisms, Feminisms and Epistemologies* (Bloomington: Indiana University Press, 1998).

11. Lorraine Code, "Taking Subjectivity into Account," in *Feminist Epistemologies*, 15–48.

12. Karl Popper, *Objective Knowledge* (Oxford: Clarendon Press, 1972), 108, cited in Code, 17.

13. S. Kierkegaard, *Samlede Værker VII, Afsluttende Uvidenskabelig Efter-skrift* (København: C. U. Reizel, 1846). English edition: *On Concluding Unscientific Postscript*, ed. Walter Lowrie, trans. D. F. Swenson and L. M. Swenson (Princeton, N.J.: Princeton University Press, 1969).

14. K. E. Løgstrup, *Ophav og Omgivelse; Betragninger over Historie og Natur; Metafysik III* (København: Gyldendal, 1976, 1995).

15. Code, 19.

16. See Evelyn Fox Keller, *Reflections on Gender and Science* (New Haven, Conn.: Yale University Press, 1984).

17. Evelyn Fox Keller, *A Feeling for the Organism: The Life and Work of Barbara McClintock* (New York: W. H. Freeman and Co., 1984).

18. Seyla Benhabib, "The Generalized and the Concrete Other," in *Feminism as Critique*, ed. Seyla Benhabib and Drucilla Cornell (Minneapolis: University of Minnesota Press, 1987), 85, cited in Code, 33.

19. See Sandra Harding, *Whose Science? Whose Knowledge?* (Ithaca, N.Y.: Cornell University Press, 1991), 150–61.

20. Code, 30.

21. Vrinda Dalmiya and Linda Alcoff, "Are 'Old Wives' Tales Justified?" in Potter and Alcoff, 217–44.

22. Dalmiya and Alcoff, 222–23.

23. Dalmiya and Alcoff reject Gilbert Ryle's project of reducing the account of knowing to knowing how. They want to add to the types of knowing that are considered legitimate. Moreover, they take the modest line of criticism to show that knowing how is linked to propositions: "the agent . . . [is] able to *recognize* conditional propositions and rules underlying her skill if and when they are formulated to her . . . and it is the latter that makes her simple skill *cognitively* relevant" (233, 236–37).

24. This can be viewed as a correlate of the view that the human and cultural sciences—the *Geisteswissenscaften*—should not be modeled on the natural sciences. If these disciplines are different in terms of the nature of the realities they study and of the methods they employ, then one should not expect the natural sciences to have the subjective, experiential qualities that characterize the human sciences. For a close discussion of these issues, see Finn Collin, *Social Reality* (Routledge: London and New York, 1997), 104–6.

25. Donna Haraway, "Situated Knowledges: The Science Question in Feminism and the Privilege of Partial Perspective," in *Simians, Cyborgs, and Women: The Reinvention of Nature* (New York: Routledge, 1991), 187.

26. Haraway, "Animal Sociology and a Natural Economy of the Body Politic: A Political Physiology of Dominance," in *Simians, Cyborgs and Women*, 16–19.

27. For the following discussion, see "Situated Knowledges," 190–98.

28. Alcoff, *Real Knowing: New Versions of the Coherence Theory* (Ithaca, N.Y.: Cornell University Press, 1996), 15–16, 118–25.

29. See, for example, Susan Hekman, *Gender and Knowledge: Elements of a Postmodern Feminism* (Boston: Northeast University Press, 1990), 9. She writes, "A postmodern approach to feminist issues entails the attempt to formulate not an 'epistemology' in the sense of a replacement of the Enlightenment conception, but, rather, an explanation of the discursive processes by which human beings gain understanding of their common world."

30. Lynn Hankinson Nelson, "Empiricism," in *A Companion to Feminist Philosophy*, ed. Alison M. Jaggar and Iris Marion Young (Oxford: Blackwell, 1998), 30–38.

31. Longino, 112–17. Longino works explicitly with a model theoretic approach to scientific knowledge, where relations and structures in a model guide our interactions and interventions in the world.

32. Nelson, "Epistemological Communities," in Alcoff and Potter, 123.

33. Nelson, 126.

34. Nancy Hartsock, "The Feminist Standpoint: Developing the Ground for a Specifically Feminist Historical Materialism," in *Discovering Reality*, ed. Sandra Harding and Merrill B. Hintikka (Dordrecht: D. Reidel, 1983). For the following discussion see 285–90.

35. See also Michele Barrett, *Women's Oppression Today: Problems in Marxist Feminist Analysis* (London: New Left Books and Verso Editions, 1980); Sheila Rowbotham, *Women's Consciousness, Man's World* (London: Penguin, 1973).

36. Hartsock, 299, 303.

37. See Bat-Ami Bar On, "Everyday Violence and Ethico-Politico Crisis," in *Daring to Be Good: Essays in Feminist Ethico-Politics*, ed. Bat-Ami Bar On and Ann Ferguson (New York: Routledge, 1998), 45–52; and Bar On, "Marginality and Epistemic Privilege," in Alcoff and Potter, 83–100.

38. Sandra Harding, "Re-thinking Standpoint Epistemology: What Is 'Strong Objectivity'?" in Alcoff and Potter, 69. See also Harding, *Whose Science? Whose Knowledge?* chapter 6 and Harding, *Is Science Multicultural: Postcolonialisms, Feminisms and Epistemologies.*

39. Harding, *Whose Science? Whose Knowledge?*, 157.

40. Sandra Harding, ed., *Feminism and Methodology* (Bloomington: Indiana University Press, 1987), 1.

41. Patricia Hill Collins, *Black Feminist Thought: Knowledge, Consciousness, and the Politics of Empowerment* (New York: Routledge, Chapman and Hall, 1990), 206.

42. Collins, 207.

43. For the following discussion and citations, see Collins, 234–36.

44. For this latter point, see Bar On's "Everyday Violence and Ethico-Political Crises" as well as Claudia Card, *The Unnatural Lottery: Character and Moral Luck* (Philadelphia: Temple University Press, 1996).

45. For the following discussion, see Alcoff, *Real Knowing*, 207–18.

46. Alcoff, *Real Knowing*, chapters 4–5.

47. Alcoff, *Real Knowing*, 58–77. There have been other thinkers on both sides of the Atlantic who have contributed to a critique of positivist conceptions of rationality, who have in varying degrees emphasized the role of intersubjectivity and community in knowledge, and who have inspired feminist debate. See, for example, Johanna Meehan, ed., *Feminists Read Habermas: Gendering the Subject of Discourse* (New York and London: Routledge, 1995) for a discussion of Habermas; Charlene Haddock Seigfried, *Pragmatism and Feminism: Reweaving the Social Fabric* (Chicago and London: University of Chicago Press, 1996), for a discussion of pragmatism.

48. Alcoff, *Real Knowing*, 219.

49. Elizabeth Grosz, "Bodies and Knowledges: Feminism and the Crisis of Reason," in Alcoff and Potter, 188, 203.

50. Luce Irigaray, *This Sex Which Is Not One*, trans. Catherine Porter (Ithaca, N.Y.: Cornell University Press, 1985), 26. See also Margaret Whitford, *Luce Irigaray: Philosophy in the Feminine* (London: Routledge, 1991), 59.

51. Irigaray, *This Sex Which Is Not One*, 78.

52. Rosi Braidotti, "Teratologies," in *Deleuze and Feminist Theory*, ed. Ian Buchanan and Claire Colebrook, 162. See also Claire Colebrook, "Introduction," 1–17 and Braidotti, *Nomadic Subjects* (New York: Columbia University Press, 1994), 111–23.

53. Immanuel Wallerstein and Celestous Juma, *Open the Social Sciences* (Stanford: Stanford University Press, 1966). Cited in Bente Rosenbeck, "Mellem subjektivitet og objektivitet," 14, manuscript.

CHAPTER THREE

~

Feminist Ethics of Conflict

We have learned that one can never say never again.

—Mirsad Tokaca, director of the Bosnian State Commission
for War Crimes Documentation Center

At the beginning of his late work "Religion within the boundaries of mere reason" (1793), Immanuel Kant outlines two models of history: One model assumes that human history is the story of a fall and decline from life in Paradise; the second model assumes that the "world stead-fastly . . . forges ahead in the opposite direction, namely from bad to better."[1] This optimistic belief in rational progress has been one of the central legacies of the Enlightenment, although historical events in the last 100 years have made it difficult to justify. There is no doubt that in terms of the sheer numbers of casualties, the tragedies of war have escalated in the twentieth century. In the years 1900–1990, there were four times as many war deaths as in the preceding four hundred years.[2] In the wake of the civil war in the former Yugoslavia and the genocide in Rwanda, issues of violence, trauma, and the concept of evil again have become urgent matters for contemporary intellectuals. The September 11 terrorist attacks on the World Trade Center and the Pentagon and the ensuing military assault in Afghanistan in the name of Enduring Freedom, bring no reassurance that an epoch of violence will soon end.

Thus, some of the most urgent ethical questions of our day deal with issues of violence and war. They are urgent for citizens of all nations and, hence, crucial for feminist philosophers to address. The goals of this chapter are therefore different from the ones in the earlier chapters. I will not discuss the antifeminist objections that have been a theme in the previous chapters. Nor will I provide an overview of debates in feminist ethics. Such an overview would include debates about an "ethics of care" and concepts of justice, concepts of autonomy and relationality, moral epistemology and the role of emotion in ethics, the proposals for maternal ethics and lesbian ethics, the contributions of eco-feminists and the responses to issues of pornography, prostitution, affirmative action, and sexual violence.[3] Instead, I will focus on the last issue, violence, and ask: What does the existence of violence in human life imply for ethical reflection? What are the ethical implications of sexual violence? Mainstream ethics does not bring the existence of violence into the heart of ethical reflection. Even when philosophers do reflect on violence, they generally do not attend to the phenomena of sexual violence. Many feminist philosophers, however, do recognize that analyses of violence and oppression are the originary impulse of feminist ethics. In this chapter I present some of my own research on the violence of war rape as one illustration of how feminist ethics can be done.

It is common practice to treat ethics as the philosophical study of morality, whereas morality refers to the concrete norms and principles by which people live their daily lives. In treating morality as the norms by which people live, one needs to include practices of awareness, responsibility, judgment, and feeling that arise in and organize interpersonal relations.[4] But this distinction between ethics and morality does not clarify their relation. Does ethics *study* norms or *set* them? Some philosophers argue that ethics sets norms through systematic reflection on rational principles that are thereby applied in daily life. One can call this the top-down approach to ethics. Other philosophers argue that ethics studies norms, examining the actual moral behavior of members of a society, to give a reflective and critical analysis of moral life. One can call this the bottom-up approach to ethics. The bottom-up approach characterizes the work of many feminist ethicists, in particular the American philosopher Margaret Urban Walker. In treating morality as an actual, as opposed to an ideal, order, one commits oneself to incorporating descriptive and empirical material in moral philosophy to a greater degree than in a top-down analysis of ethics.

In the bottom-up approach to ethics, one needs to account for not only the way in which people abide by certain norms but also for the way they fail to abide by them, or the ways norms themselves become radically altered so that they undermine the possibility of coexistence. The bottom-up approach to ethics enables one to take seriously the element of conflict in human affairs. One faces the need of supplementing traditional normative questions about how one ought to act in the face of conflict, with questions about how conflicts are generated. Hence, the bottom-up approach to ethics implies that philosophers need to reflect on specific dilemmas in human life, instead of merely hypothetical or fictive dilemmas. Philosophers, including feminist ones, who take up this challenge contribute to rethinking fundamental concepts of the moral subject, moral knowledge, and responsibility.

The bottom-up approach to ethics, which anchors philosophical ethics in reflection on historical crises, does not view ethics as providing a justification of universal foundational principles that are applied to specific situations. Theorists who situate ethics in concrete contexts want to explore a broad range of moral phenomena, including: How were German soldiers able to treat extermination in the Nazi death camps as business as usual? How can individuals commit murder and still consider themselves moral, as Adolf Eichmann did when he claimed to live by Kant's moral precept while carrying out the Final Solution?[5] How can both individuals and collectivities participate in mass forgetting of moral principles? How can one make ethical judgments about perpetrators, victims, and those who live in a "gray zone," where complicity ensures survival?[6] Philosophical ethics must consider both how norms organize individual and social behavior, as well as how norms become reconfigured in periods of social transition. When one views morality as the practices that guide people's lives, one widens the discussion of morality to include elements of moral psychology (e.g., moral feelings) and elements of social theory (e.g., the role of social breakdown in moral transformation).

Hence, this bottom-up approach includes a descriptive dimension of ethics, contrary to philosophers who argue that description in ethics is only a disguise for doing sociology, history, or psychology. Hannah Arendt, one of the leading philosophers of the twentieth century, was for many years treated as a political scientist instead of as a philosopher because of her work on totalitarianism and on Eichmann's trial. But her work *Eichmann in Jerusalem* is philosophical, not only because it is "a philosopher's discussion of general philosophical questions as reflected in one particular case; but because just this particularity is the route philosophy must take if it is to understand the nature of judgment."[7]

The top-down approach to ethics, which rejects the role of description in ethics, divides the world into facts and values, as do many epistemologists. For the typical moral philosopher, facts are viewed as prior to and independent of interpretations, and norms are viewed as independent of contexts. Kant epitomizes this position in arguing that descriptive analysis of human motivation played no part in moral philosophy. Such descriptive analysis belongs instead to practical anthropology, or what today might be termed the social sciences. Kant contrasts practical anthropology with morality, where actions are determined by the rational will alone, not by inclination. But how can one know that one acts from will rather than from inclination? How can one know that one effectively controls one's inclinations? And if one cannot answer these questions satisfactorily, how can one know whether moral behavior is ever possible?

Kant's model distinguishes empirical consciousness from prescriptive consciousness and denies that empirical consciousness is imbued with aims and values that give meaning to the empirical world. In my own work on Kant I have proposed a critical feminist reading, drawing inspiration from philosophers like G. W. F. Hegel, Karl Marx, and Maurice Merleau-Ponty who refuse to separate out value components from knowledge of the empirical world.[8] If one rejects the fact–value dichotomy, then it is necessary to rethink the job of the moral philosopher. French existentialist philosophers like Merleau-Ponty, Jean-Paul Sartre, and Simone de Beauvoir propose an alternative approach to ethics, which understands norms as constituting empirical phenomena as well as providing ideals that people strive to attain. The existentialist approach to ethics does not undermine norms but it does undermine the claim that norms are pure, context independent, and incorrigible. Existentialist ethics situates norms in the contexts in which they originate and finds the criteria for either justifying or challenging specific norms within these contexts. This approach supports what I call the bottom-up approach to ethics, which maintains a commitment to descriptive analysis as part of the job of ethics. In relation to issues of violence, the existentialist approach implies that one can only meaningfully discuss how norms should be applied in situations of violence, if one understands how violence is generated and how specific moral practices may be complicitous in reproducing violence.[9]

But the reader may ask, What does this discussion about descriptive and normative work have to do with feminist analyses of ethics? Feminist ethicists challenge the fact–value divide and the separation between moral and social practices to argue for the role of empirical knowledge in moral reflection. Many feminist ethicists consider analyses of and resistance to oppression and violence a central task for feminism and, hence, for ethical reflection as well. In her book *Moral Understandings*, Margaret Urban Walker defines morality as follows: "I take morality to consist in complex practices of certain kinds in complexly differentiated social orders and individually varied lives. . . . Moral theorizing . . . can directly interrogate some of the most morally troubling aspects of human social life: domination, oppression, exclusion, coercion, and basic disregard of some people by others."[10] Walker's work is specifically feminist in that it is inspired by the political critique of gender inequalities that was spawned in the 1960s and that developed into a critique of gender bias in theoretical representations. She criticizes prevailing tendencies in contemporary ethical theory, which treat the moral agent as one who is not a woman, child, or person marked by a specific ethnic, racial, or religious identity and not a person who is dependent on others for survival. As Walker notes, "this moral agent is none of us at all times, and many of us at no times."[11] But this failure to situate the moral agent results in philosophers' idealizing aspects of the actual positions of some individuals in a social order as if they were neutral, and in overlooking the significance of power relations among moral agents. Along with her challenge to the concept of the moral agent, Walker challenges the tendency to treat ethics as a codifiable set of formulas that can be applied by any agent in any situation.[12]

In situating ethics, feminist theorists focus on concrete issues of oppression and violence that have been a central concern for feminist political movements. Unfortunately, violence against women is an enduring feature of the present. Hence, as the American political theorist Linda Bell writes, feminist ethics "must anchor itself in the reality of violence, oppression, and colonization in order to offer adequate moral critiques."[13] Feminist ethicists offer descriptive and critical analyses about how violence and oppression distort moral character and violate moral relations, and they offer alternative theories for conceptualizing moral goals. Feminist philosophers do not exclusively focus on violence against women, but it serves as an important test for theories.

Feminists analyze ethics within the context of gender, race, and class relations. Many of these contributions retain the traditional definition of ethics as fundamentally concerned with standards of good character and right action. More recently, however, there is work that focuses on ethics from the intersection of feminist and poststructuralist theory. This work makes at least two crucial contributions. First, although poststructuralist theorists argue that universals cannot operate as rigid or foundational principles, they propose a strategic concept of universality that is constantly being renegotiated in specific situations. The decision in 2001 by the International Criminal Tribunal for the former Yugoslavia, which condemned three Bosnian Serb soldiers for rape and crimes against humanity, can be viewed as one illustration of the strategic character of universality. Judge Florence Mumba argued that a crime had been committed against a general feature of humanity, but she framed her judgment in terms of women's specific right to sexual consent.[14] Second, some theorists influenced by poststructuralism point to the concepts of antagonism and conflict as ineradicable elements of human existence and, hence, of ethical relations. For example, the Polish-American theorist Ewa Ziarek points to the conflict between freedom and obligation as a constitutive tension in ethics.[15] By this she means that one may have obligations that one has not freely chosen. From a feminist poststructuralist perspective, ethics is an inquiry into human subjectivity, a subjectivity that suffers from internal splits and contradictions, is motivated by desire and ambivalence, and is immutably embodied. Some feminist philosophers and theorists of race analyze ethical terms such as responsibility in relation to concepts of conflict, ambivalence, alterity, and embodiment. This work shifts the task of ethical inquiry away from investigating moral principles as primary to focus on analyses of moral subjectivity and moral phenomenology.

In this chapter, I will discuss questions that have arisen in my own work in feminist ethics. (1) What are the conceptual strategies that are available for analyzing the central role of conflict, ambiguity, and ambivalence in human affairs? Here I have found it particularly useful to draw on the work of Simone de Beauvoir, one of the most important women philosophers of the twentieth century and a key figure for contemporary feminist theorists.[16] (2) How does a philosophical analysis of empirical examples of conflict and violence add to an understanding of ethics? Here I will draw on material about the war rapes during the civil wars in the former Yugoslavia. (3) What concepts are available for understanding the constructive moment of ethics, in which the work of healing and restoration must take place? Here I will discuss the concepts of recognition and witnessing that feminist theorists have debated.

Simone de Beauvoir and the Ethics of Negativity

Simone de Beauvoir works within an existentialist approach to philosophy, and her work is linked to philosophers such as Martin Heidegger, Jean-Paul Sartre, and Maurice Merleau-Ponty. Beauvoir focuses on the paradoxes and contradictions at the heart of human relations, themes that later poststructuralist theorists have emphasized. In this section, I will present some of Beauvoir's key contributions to thinking about the ethical implications of human ambiguities and contradictions, which I will draw on in the subsequent discussion of war rape.

In her book *The Ethics of Ambiguity*, Beauvoir makes what is perhaps the only sustained attempt by any of these thinkers to work through the ethical implications of existentialism, which she does through a discussion of terms such as paradox, negativity, and ambiguity. In the opening of her book she writes that existentialism is "the only philosophy in which ethics has a place."[17] By this she means that existentialism is the only philosophy that takes seriously the element of paradox and negativity in human existence. Human existence is fundamentally paradoxical, as is evident in the fact that humans have consciousness and intentionality, but they cannot escape their natural condition, cannot escape being an object or instrument for others, and ultimately are fated to die. Thus, failure is an inescapable element of the human condition. Our life projects are frustrated by our natural condition both during our lives and through our deaths.

Failure is immanent in the structure of human freedom, and it is human failure that makes ethics meaningful. Beauvoir views the questions of freedom as primary to human subjectivity and, hence, views human subjectivity as primarily an ethical existence. In her view, there is an inherent split or alienation in human existence, which makes possible different relations to freedom, e.g., the escape from freedom or its affirmation. One can never completely flee from freedom, nor can affirming one's freedom overcome the primary split or alienation within human existence. Hence, human existence is constituted by the tension between these different ethical possibilities.

Beauvoir's analysis presents moral subjectivity as relational, a term that has become central in contemporary feminist discussions of the self and of autonomy.[18] Moral subjectivity for Beauvoir consists, on one level, of the relation within the internally split subject, a relation that can be the source of self-alienation. On another level, moral subjectivity for Beauvoir must be understood in terms of interpersonal relations. Beauvoir describes the me–others relationship as fundamental to human existence.[19] Only by understanding the oppositional character of interpersonal relations can social conflicts become comprehensible. Beauvoir follows Hegel in viewing conflict between me and others as an expression of interdependency. The simultaneity of interdependence and opposition explains why oppression exists and why it is hateful. Although the oppositional–interdependency structure of human relations is a condition for the existence of division and violence, oppression and enslavement are not inevitable. If individuals recognize each other in a reciprocal manner, oppression and enslavement can be overcome. I will return to the notion of reciprocal recognition in the concluding section of this chapter. Beauvoir acknowledges that the struggle for reciprocal recognition will never cease and is a struggle that leaves individuals always in danger in their relation with their fellows.[20]

Thus Beauvoir's approach to moral subjectivity leaves us with the following insights: (1) Moral subjectivity and intersubjectivity are relational affairs. (2) Conflict is inevitable both internal to the moral subject and between subjects. (3) Hence, failure is an inevitable dimension of moral subjectivity. (4) Consequently, an understanding of the conditions, acts, and temptations that lead to failure are an essential part of ethical reflection. It is this approach to moral subjectivity that paves the way for an analysis of social institutions as an essential part of the project of ethics. Social institutions, which, for example, legitimize racism and sexism, provide the conditions for moral failure. Analyzing the social injuries of racism and sexism that contribute to moral failure will not eliminate the wounds of existence altogether. But this approach seeks to alleviate rather than aggravate these wounds by maximizing the possibilities for human freedom.

In *The Ethics of Ambiguity*, Beauvoir develops a moral phenomenology that analyzes the complex postures by which individuals embrace their freedom, renounce their freedom, or embrace their freedom through its renunciation, as in the example of the sixteen-year-old Nazi who died crying, "Heil Hitler!"[21] Her book *America Day by Day* continues this project by tracing the attitudes toward race she met among whites and blacks during her four-month journey through America in 1947. The book is dedicated to her friends Ellen and Richard Wright, who were her hosts in New York, and gives evidence of the significance for Beauvoir of Richard Wright's analysis of the subjective experience of racial oppression.[22] In this work, she couples moral phenomenology with an analysis of social institutions, specifically institutions that legitimize racism. The book makes two significant contributions to ethics. (1) By connecting moral failure with social institutions that aggravate this failure, Beauvoir develops moral phenomenology into a phenomenology of oppression—a notion developed by Richard Wright. (2) Beauvoir implies that an individualistic perspective in ethics is incomplete. Ethical analysis must incorporate features typically excluded from an individualistic-based ethics, with its focus on individuals' intentions, actions, or principles. Instead, ethics must incorporate analyses of social institutions and historical developments to make moral judgments that can transcend the ambiguity of individual moral attitudes. Beauvoir approached the problem of sexual oppression in *The Second Sex* (1949), with its focus both on the details of daily life and the overarching features of patriarchy, in a manner analogous to her discussion of racism in *America Day by Day*.

A phenomenology of oppression traces the political dimension of relations between individuals. It focuses on the subjective landscape of oppression, as it is revealed in relations between oppressors and oppressed. Beauvoir describes her method in *The Ethics of Ambiguity* as "confronting the values realized with the values aimed at, and the meaning of the act with its content."[23] This method becomes a tool for analyzing the contradictions in the attitudes of those who deprive others of freedom (e.g., racists, anti-Semites, misogynists). Her analysis resonates with that of her contemporaries, not only with Richard Wright's *Native Son* (1940) but also Jean-Paul Sartre's *Anti-Semite and Jew* (*Réflexions sur la question juive*, 1946) and Frantz Fanon's *Black Skin, White Masks* (*Peau noire, masques blancs*, 1952).

In *America Day by Day* Beauvoir analyzes racism both as a problem for whites and for blacks. For whites, the problem lies in their attitude toward themselves, in their self-hatred and fear that leads them to project onto blacks images of animal sensuality and naturalness. According to Beauvoir, whites of the lower ranks of the social hierarchy use their racial privileges to feel superiority over *somebody*, and in this way they do not try to improve their own position.[24] Whites rationalize their view that blacks *are* inferior by reference to the so-called given, natural features of race, failing to understand that this is a situation that has evolved. The arrogant hatred of whites does not prevent them from having an attitude of ambivalence toward blacks. Though white southerners would never eat at the same table as blacks, they eat the food blacks have prepared and entrust their own children to the care of blacks.[25]

In describing the attitude of blacks, Beauvoir follows Wright's injunction that for blacks every moment of their lives is penetrated by the social consciousness of being black. The consciousness of blacks is always framed by what "black" means in a world in which norms established by white people are dominant. Blacks are forced to live with a double face, a split consciousness. On the one hand, blacks put on a mask for white people and maintain the appearance of happy laughter. On the other hand, blacks maintain a silent hatred of whites because of the economic and political inequalities that entrap them.

Beauvoir's phenomenology of oppression has several implications for ethics. (1) The kind of moral failure that is evident in racial oppression is part of everyday realities. Hence, moral failure does not belong to some abstract other that is responsible for evil, whereas I/we are responsible for good. For Beauvoir, good and evil are not distinct and opposing categories. The tendency in American culture to polarize good and evil results from a denial of the complexity of problems and a belief that there are some completely innocent or virtuous solutions. Beauvoir's analysis shows that the moral failure of racism, which she calls evil, is part of human attitudes and actions, whether one is on the side of the oppressor or the oppressed. (2) We live the moral failure implicit in unfree social situations through our bodies. As Beauvoir illustrates in *America Day by Day*, evil is present in the way in which a white woman treats a black woman in a segregated bus and in the way in which a black jazz musician hears the applause of the white audience, knowing that he would not be welcome to sit with them. The glance of the white woman on the bus, her stiffness in walking past the black woman, the sound of distancing applause in the jazz club—these are all embodiments of a moral failure to recognize the freedom of other persons.

Thus, social institutions and practices such as racial discrimination in the United States are complicitous in moral failure. Beauvoir criticizes these institutions indirectly in the phenomenology of oppression, which examines what these institutions *do* to people. She also criticizes them directly, as when she refers to both poverty and racial oppression as "evils."[26] Implicit here is the view that to make moral judgments, it is not adequate to merely analyze the logic of individual action. Systematic forms of oppression—such as lynching in the southern United States, the Nazi extermination camps, the Soviet labor camps, the public disclosure of which shocked Beauvoir's circle of left-leaning French intellectuals who had fought with the Resistance—cannot be understood as a compilation of individual acts. It is also crucial to examine the pattern, organization, and purpose of these forms of oppression and to make judgments about specific social projects. The moral analysis of individual agents' attitudes and actions must be supplemented in ethics by an analysis of the logic of social practices. Judgments about social practices do not escape the problem of fallibility. Beauvoir at first defended the Soviet camps, because she viewed them as part of a historical project that improved the lot of the mass of people, and later recanted on her early judgment. But the fallibility of judgment does not override her crucial contribution, that analyses of the effects of specific social institutions on moral behavior are a necessary dimension of philosophical ethics. Beauvoir's situated approach to ethics makes a crucial contribution to contemporary feminist discussions. It is from this perspective that analysis of the particular form of oppression that takes place in war rape, which I discuss below, becomes a crucial project for feminist ethics.

In addition to Beauvoir's focus on *individual* behavior and attitudes and on how ethics is *socially situated*, she focuses on the *cultural* dimension of ethics. Ethics must also address the nature of the symbolic representations that organize what Beauvoir calls our dreams, fears, and idols. Her emphasis on the patterns of meanings embodied in symbols that are used to reproduce a culture resonates profoundly with contemporary discussions. For example, the American philosopher Virginia Held, in her book *Feminist Morality*, views the analysis and transformation of cultural images and metaphors as one of the central tasks of feminist ethics.[27]

For Beauvoir, the analysis of the cultural dimension of ethics is anchored in her analysis of otherness. In phenomenological analysis of consciousness, such as Hegel's, every consciousness sets itself up as the essential, as opposed to the other, and the other sets up a reciprocal claim to define itself as essential.[28] But in cultural relations between the sexes, this reciprocity is lacking; woman becomes the Other. Beauvoir explicitly links this representation of woman as Other with the representation of evil. She writes of Eve and Pandora, "The Other— she is passivity confronting activity, diversity that destroys unity, matter as opposed to form, disorder against order. Woman is thus dedicated to Evil." And woman "incarnates all moral values, from good to evil, and their opposites."[29] In these passages, Beauvoir is suggesting a logic of instability in symbolic representations. When representations of woman as Other become part of a dualistic conceptual system based on the concepts of good and evil, there is an instability within the system that drives each concept to turn into its opposite. Thus, woman is "pitiable, hateful, sinful, victimized, coquettish, weak, angelic, devilish."[30] The representation of women by these contradictory characteristics cannot be explained by the complexities of female psychology alone. But it can be explained by the logic of opposing concepts, which shows how ambivalent representations of women become sedimented in culture, despite or even because of their contradictory character.[31] Thus, the cultural dimension of ethics must examine the contradictory nature of representations that sustain the identification of "others" with evil.

The individual, social, and cultural levels of ethical analysis are not merely descriptive but are also part of the normative work of ethics. In pointing to the contradictions of individual moral attitudes, the call to individual freedom resonates. In pointing to the social dimensions of moral phenomena, the call for social emancipation is echoed. The social situatedness of this ethical approach transgresses what is sometimes an artificial divide between ethics and politics. And in pointing to the cultural dimension of moral representations, one challenges the way in which polarized moral values, e.g., good and evil, sustain existing social hierarchies and, thus, one begins a reconceptualization of these terms.

Ethical Analyses of War Rape and Sexual Torture

The atrocities of war rape have reached new levels of public awareness, but the phenomenon is hardly new. A recent book by the British military historian Antony Beevor documents that the Red Army was responsible for raping up to two million women during World War II.[32] A new way of writing history, one that is involved with the emotional details of a reality under siege, has made visible a phenomenon that previously has been treated as invisible. The war rapes in the civil wars in the former Yugoslavia became particularly visible to me because I had traveled in the country, met my Danish husband in Dubrovnik, made friends who later were personally affected by the wars, being dislocated or involved in local resistance. My professional interests included analysis of philosophical representations of female sexuality, motherhood, and war. After hearing Claudia Card's lecture on "Rape as a Weapon of War" at the University of Copenhagen in 1996, I was inspired to study the war rapes in Bosnia-Herzegovina and Croatia (1991–1995). Working with this material creates dread and nausea and the need to find conceptual tools that can honor the complexity of subjective moral experience and the irreducible corporality of these moral transgressions. In this context, I have found it useful to work with the concepts of moral phenomenology, analyses of how institutions structure moral transgression, and analyses of the logic of symbolic systems, which are implicit in Beauvoir's work.

With this work, I seek to show the urgency for ethics of confronting contemporary forms of violence. Ethics needs a multidimensional analysis that bypasses controversies about whether it is most important to study the personal dimension, the institutional analysis, or the analysis of symbolic forms.[33] All of these mediations are required to address the ethical problems posed by this form of violence. In reading material on war rapes and other forms of sexual torture, one may well reach what the Italian poet Zanzotto calls "the politics of continuous vomiting."[34] Beverly Allen, author of *Rape Warfare*, reached her breaking point after hearing that in one rape–death camp the women were being raped on bloody sheets. She heard that the sheets were bloody because they were spread over cots that had been used during the torture of male prisoners, including relatives and friends of the women victims. Having believed that this was her darkest moment, she later heard that the bloody sheets were not sheets at all. They were bloody rags, rags that the women had used each day to mop up blood in the room where amputations and tortures had taken place the night before. This, Allen describes, wrecked her final defenses and forced her to accept that things were far, far worse than she had believed.[35]

I reached my breaking point when I read about a woman who was a survivor of multiple rapes in one of the camps, whose husband had rejected and divorced her, and who had remarried. But the new marriage was haunted by a dangerous cycle of sadomasochistic violence in which the husband and wife continually exchanged roles of the victim and tormentor. Although they had a child together, the violence was so destructive that it was impossible for the partners to rear the child. This example, far from isolated, shows the enduring effects of post-torture trauma among survivors.[36]

Although there is a radical difference in degree between the emotional intensity and physical harm present in everyday discrimination and the harm caused by violent attack, the conditions at work in the former are also present in the latter. Both Wright and Beauvoir focus on how political relations of oppression frame the subjective content of everyday racial interactions. Political relations between dominant and subordinate groups frame the subjective experience of extreme situations as well. But what strategies are available for describing the attitudes of victims and perpetrators? How can one avoid giving a compilation of victims' testimony or a fictive narrative of generalizable features? In what follows, I extend Beauvoir's methodology to offer an alternative to these two options. Beauvoir's method is phenomenological in focusing on the lived experience of both partners in a moral relation or moral transgression. This analysis includes at least two dimensions: an analysis of the logic of attitudes and an analysis of the corporality of experience. In the following, I discuss testimony given both by men who have been convicted of rape and murder during wartime and by women who have been victims of rape or attempted rape. I show the internal contradictions in the logic of the perpetrators' attitudes and the way they experienced their actions corporally. I also examine the way in which the life projects of the victims are undermined and how these women's corporeal experience of themselves becomes transformed through these acts of violence. I also consider the institutional and symbolic parameters of these transgressions, which also must be considered a form of violence.

Rape is an act of violence and humiliation that destroys the victim's sense of self and her trust in the world and in ordinary human relations. The Greek-Danish psychologist Libby Tata Arcel, who for two and a half years led a psychosocial treatment program in Zagreb for Bosnian torture and war victims under the auspices of the International Rehabilitation Council for Torture Victims, defines rape as:

> Forcible penetration or near-penetration (vaginal, rectal, oral) of a woman's body openings by body parts of or any instruments used by

a person in official capacity during armed conflict or during peace with the purpose of manifesting aggression and causing physical and psychological damage. Rape includes cases where a woman is coerced to exchange sexual favors for certain entitlements for herself or her family (food, necessary papers, health services) or is coerced to sexual intercourse because she fears for her safety.[37]

Arcel notes that other forms of sexual assault (e.g., forcing women to take part in unnatural sexual relations with family members or animals or other captives, inflicting pain or mutilation on the genitals or breasts, forced witnessing of rape, forced masturbation, sexual threats, molestation without penetration) are equivalent to rape in a psychological sense. Estimates of the numbers of women raped during the war range from twenty thousand to fifty thousand and although the majority of victims were of childbearing age, victims also included young children (e.g., a four-year-old girl[38]) and women in their seventies. Although it is impossible to know how many women were impregnated because of rape, one small-scale study showed that 10 percent of victims who sought help had become pregnant.[39]

War rape is part of a widespread pattern of violence linked to explicit military strategy. Sexualized violence in wartime is not unique to the civil wars in the former Yugoslavia. There is substantial literature that attends to the ways in which military practices have been used to define masculinity and to express misogynist and homophobic attitudes in military speech and practice. Sara Ruddick, who writes on maternal thinking and peace politics, describes this militaristic stance as follows: "The 'monstrous male, loud of voice, hard of fist' who goes off to war singing of the 'Persian pukes' he is ready to 'nape,' the faggot assholes he is ready to sodomize, the dead and diseased whore he is ready to rape, expresses even as he caricatures this common military attitude."[40]

According to the UN Commission of Experts, the war rapes in the former Yugoslavia follow five patterns of rape, regardless of the ethnicity of the perpetrators or the victims. (1) Sexual violence occurred before widespread fighting broke out in a particular region. (2) Sexual violence occurred during fighting, attacking a town and raping or assaulting women in their homes. (3) Sexual violence occurred in detention facilities. Men were tortured or executed or sent off to work camps, while women were sent to separate camps. Soldiers, camp guards, paramilitaries, and civilians raped or sexually assaulted many of the women and frequently also murdered them. Gang rapes occurred frequently and were accompanied by beatings and other forms of humiliation. (4) Sexual violence occurred in rape camps established in hotels, schools, restaurants, hospitals, factories, brothels, barns, and auditoriums. Frequently, Serbian captors told women that they would create "Chetnik babies." Women who became pregnant were detained until it was too late to get an abortion. (5) Sexual violence occurred in bordello camps, where women provided sex for men returning from the front lines. Many of these women were killed.[41] All parties to the conflict have been guilty of these atrocities. Although the majority of the victims were Bosnian women, this does not diminish the cruelty toward or suffering of the Serbian women who also were raped and tortured.

What attitudes among the perpetrators could motivate such cruel torture? As Beauvoir points out with regard to racism, the perpetrator is filled with hatred, and the logic of hatred is paradoxical. It requires that the perpetrator abstract from the concrete identity of the other and view the other as the source of all wrongs in existence, to resolve the perpetrator's own contradictory attitudes. In the situation of wartime atrocities, this logic is motivated by the belief that the others are deserving of hatred—e.g., that the Muslim women are slime (*Balija*), that the Croatian women are fascist (*Ustasha*),[42] that the men have been plotting to kidnap and murder Serbian children. According to this logic, there is something wrong with Muslims that makes them hateful (just as in other contexts Jews or blacks are blamed). The others, e.g., the Muslims, are retaliated against for acts that they purportedly were about to commit, though they had not actually committed them. The fervor of justice becomes directed not against actual acts and their consequences, as takes place in a court of law, but against imaginary acts that might take place in the future. The attitude of the perpetrator rebels against the temporal distinctions between past, present, and future to unite all wrongs by virtue of the enduring essence of the hated group. This logic implicitly objectifies the hated others. The women who are raped and tortured can no longer be viewed as like one's own mother or sister or daughter. If one acknowledges this possible likeness, it is no longer possible to maintain this attitude of violence. One twenty-one-year-old Muslim spoke to the commander who had ordered her to be undressed. "I asked him if he had a sister. He said yes. Then I asked, 'How do you think your sister would feel if someone did with her what you're doing to me?' He jumped up and ordered me to get dressed and leave. . . . He said I didn't need to be afraid, that no one would come get me anymore, and after that no one else did come."[43]

In objectifying the other, one abstracts from their concrete individual features of identity. One twenty-two-year-old Serbian man, condemned to death by a military court in Sarajevo, said that he did not know how many girls he had raped, how many were killed afterward, or what their names were. He describes all his victims as the same, "tall, dark-haired, and between twenty and twenty-five years of age."[44] This objectification and abstraction was facilitated when perpetrators did not come from the same area as their victims. Thus, foreign Serbs were more likely to use excessive violence against Muslims than local Serbs. One forty-five-year-old woman said, "The local Serbs, they went easier, they weren't so extreme. But as soon as the foreigner came . . . then they had pressure on them and you knew they just had to do it."[45] Yet personal rage can also be used to justify objectifying attitudes. The human rights expert Kelly Dawn Askin writes, "In this conflict, neighbors have raped neighbors, friends have raped friends, teachers have raped students. . . . In the Yugoslav conflict, there have been allegations that atrocities have been committed not just against the official 'enemy' but against a soldier or commander's *personal* enemy."[46] Everyday feelings of envy, jealousy, hurt pride, or humiliation became transformed in the atmosphere of hatred into a brutal authorization of force. The personal enemy—e.g., who had rejected one, who had uncomfortable authority over one—became a physical enemy to be manipulated and abused.

The fear that motivates hateful acts is not merely fear of the other group, e.g., Muslims. It may also be a fear of one's own group—the literal threats of murder or castration (sometimes carried out) or humiliation if a man does not comply in committing violence. The men who committed violence unwillingly are also victims of violence, and they experienced a terrible realization that committing acts of rape and murder, even if unwillingly, have the effect of increasing hatred and destroying bonds with members of the victims' group. Thus, the logic of hatred relies on the logic of group identity. Individual Muslims are seen first and foremost as manifesting a collective identity as Muslims, by which their fate is justified. Meanwhile, the perpetrators' acts are not only motivated by virtue of their own ethnic or national identity but are directly enabled by virtue of the group action—as evidenced in the widespread use of gang rapes. Thus, the perpetrators subordinate themselves to a group identity, just as they do to their victims.

The desire involved in those who commit rape under these conditions is most often not a sexual desire at all. Rather, the act is a sexualized manifestation of aggression.[47] The desire that motivates sexualized aggression may be a desire to avoid one's own humiliation, irrespective of the consequences for one's victims. One twenty-three-year-old Serbian who killed over eighty Croatians and Muslims and raped several girls said, "The soldiers told me I should rape her, and the others too. . . . But I was afraid, and I didn't have an erection. They egged me on, and I had to take down my pants and lie down on top of her. . . . I had absolutely no feeling for what I was doing . . . and then I did get an erection, but I didn't feel anything. I didn't come." Another soldier said, "I didn't feel anything while I was doing it, it was only a little, each one a little bit . . . it didn't excite me at all."[48] Thus, the logic of hating sets up a perversion of the Golden Rule, whereby the unwilling perpetrator does unto others (physical and psychological humiliation) what he fears will be done to himself.

In some men, however, the desire involved in rape does express a sadistic pleasure in cruelty to others so as to promote their own self-importance.[49] One Muslim woman who had been raped in her apartment, with her four-year-old daughter watching, said, "They came and went, they drank and smoked marijuana. They laughed, they had fun."[50] This deliberate infliction of violence with malevolent intent gives rise to the most extreme form of trauma in the survivors.[51]

In all of these attitudes of hatred, the perpetrator ends up subordinating himself to the same categories of thought that he applies to his victims. In viewing the other as hateful and deserving of a justice that ignores temporal distinctions, the perpetrator himself ends up committing the violent acts that he fears. His actions earn him the hatred of his victims—a hatred that might also lead to future transgenerational revenge—and in many cases to his own self-hatred. In objectifying the other as an indifferent physical thing to be manipulated, he leaves himself with an emptiness of feeling. ("I didn't feel anything.") In fearing the other as a member of an enemy group, he subjects himself via fear to the manipulation of his own group. In seeking to humiliate the other to avoid his own humiliation, he does not escape his own potential humiliation in front of the group. This hatred projects that which is feared and threatening onto the others and becomes inverted into the self. Hence, Julia Kristeva's injunction in *Strangers to Ourselves* to "confront that 'demon,' that threat, that apprehension generated by the projective apparition of the other at the heart of what we persist in maintaining as a proper, solid 'us.'"[52] Only by acknowledging what is threatening as an element of one's own identity can one avoid the violent logic of projection. The difference between how these self-contradictory attitudes are manifest in the everyday violence of discrimination and in the extreme violence of atrocities is explained by Arcel by the fact that violence is "allowed."[53] It is allowed because the political ideologies of nationalism and the military authorization of "ethnic cleansing" have replaced the ordinary rule of law with the active encouragement of violence.

Whereas the perpetrators themselves become subordinated to the categories of hate that they direct toward the other, the victims suffer enduring marks of the dehumanizing acts committed upon their bodies. The possibility of carrying out their everyday life projects, which anchor their identity and their freedom, becomes radically jeopardized. Several women in villages noted that they had been too busy with everyday affairs—taking care of children, washing, cooking—to pay attention to politics until soldiers came to their village. When war became a personal reality for the women who survived, their ability to carry out their everyday tasks was undermined, and their feeling of their body and of their personal relations became profoundly transformed.[54]

Victims of sexual torture experience a profound humiliation through the acts of torture. During shorter or longer periods, depending on the nature of the torture, a woman could no longer decide when to go to the bathroom, when to sleep, whether to engage in sexual acts, how to care for her children; instead, she was wholly subject to the will of another. As such, she was deprived of the feeling of being a person able to determine basic aspects of her own life. She became temporarily for herself what she was for the torturer—a physical thing vulnerable to manipulation. The extreme feeling of powerlessness and humiliation was exacerbated if the rapes were committed in front of her children, husband, or father, as often happened. The woman's own body became the occasion for a multiple violation of taboos (as in the woman whose fourteen-year-old son was forced to rape her).[55] Subsequent feelings of guilt may in part be a defensive belief that she had maintained some control and could have influenced events. The feeling of guilt may lie partly in the knowledge that her own bodily violation constitutes a threat to the order that gave meaning and coherence to her life. Through these experiences of sexual violation, women often feel that a foreign body has lodged itself in their real body and taken it over. Thus, the projection of the perpetrator— that she is the foreign element that must be excised—becomes mirrored in her own experience in an inverted fashion. There is indeed foreignness in her, but this foreignness is itself the scar left by the perpetrator. Thus, a woman may feel that an evil has moved into her body, which continues to torture her long after the actual physical torture ceases. Jean Améry, the Austrian-born Jew who survived torture and Auschwitz, writes similarly of the permanence of torture: "Whoever was tortured, stays tortured. Torture is ineradicably burned into him, even when no clinically objective traces can be detected."[56] The feeling that the raped woman's body is colonized by an evil, foreign element may express itself in somatic symptoms, such as in an inability to become pregnant. Thus, the threats during torture that she will never be able to be a woman again, that she will never be able to have children, become actualized. One woman abused in a bordello near Brcko asked a gynecologist to extirpate her generative organs, to free herself of her memories.[57] Healing requires in some sense being able to take the evil out of her body.

Sexual torture specifically involves the intimate parts of the body and, thus, may create a tormenting feeling of complicity in the victim.[58] All bodily orifices symbolize specially vulnerable points[59] for the individual person and for society—and indeed all orifices were used as a venue for attack. Many women did not experience rape as a specifically sexual form of torture but viewed it as one aspect of a multilevel trauma—which may have included witnessing the rape of young daughters, sisters, mothers or the murder of sons, husbands, fathers, or fathers-in-law. And in fact one goal in treating victims is to desexualize the act of rape to free their sexuality from these traumatic scars. Yet there is a paradox in the sexual nature of this violence. On the one hand, there is no sexual desire involved in this act—this is obvious for the woman who is attacked, but as the examples mentioned above indicate, it is true of many perpetrators as well. Hence, rape may be experienced as simply violence, not sexual violence. On the other hand, the violence does threaten to live on in her sexual life, since her most intimate, vulnerable bodily parts have been (often repeatedly) abused. The American philosopher Susan Brison describes how violence committed on the basis of sex shatters the connections between sex and love and undermines one's pleasurable erotic associations.[60] In the case of war rape and its effects, a woman may experience ongoing sexual disturbances, as in the examples of a woman's somatic inability to conceive or her participation in sadomasochistic sexual relations years after the physical torture itself has ended, where she gives her will to the objectification that she had earlier undergone against her will.[61]

In the wake of these dehumanizing acts, a woman may experience that objects and goals that had occupied her as a free woman now become meaningless; they shrink in comparison with the intensity of the experience of powerlessness. This powerlessness is more extreme for victims of torture than for victims of natural disaster. In the former case, pain was inflicted intentionally on the woman, thus undermining her trust in the world and in her relations with other human beings. The loss of control of her own body and its complete subjugation to the control of another leads to profound shame, a primal feeling connected with the loss of self-control over one's body. This shame is also connected to the cultural judgment that marks a raped woman as shameful. Shame is closely connected to feelings of rage at the loss of control of one's body. In severe trauma, the internalized images of the body, the self, and others, and of the values and ideals that give coherence to one's world, are systematically invaded and broken down.[62] Indeed, these acts of violence realize the perpetrators' collective fan-

tasy that sex can be a transformative process.[63] But instead of transforming an impure Muslim into a pure Serb, it has transformed a
woman who was at home in her body into a homeless being. For, as
the Serbian feminist and antiwar activist Lepa Mladjenovic writes,
rape makes a woman "homeless in her own body."[64]

A woman's relation to her body and to her world becomes even
more profoundly transformed when she becomes pregnant as a consequence of rape. Forced impregnation was part of the Serbian military
strategy during the civil wars in Yugoslavia. One woman who was
raped every other day by several men at a women's camp in Doboj
was told, "Come on now, if you could have *Ustasha* babies, then you
can have a Chetnick baby, too." She related, "Women who got pregnant, they had to stay there for seven or eight months so they could
give birth to a Serbian kid. They had their gynecologists there to examine the women. The pregnant ones were separated off from us and
had special privileges; they got meals, they were better off, they were
protected. Only when a woman's in her seventh month, when she
can't do anything about it anymore, then she's released."[65] For the
woman who has been impregnated through rape, the objectification
that she had experienced becomes replicated in her feelings toward
the pregnancy—a foreign thing in her belly. The UN commission that
investigated the women's clinics in January 1993 found that out of 119
pregnancies that resulted from rape, 104 women chose abortion. One
woman who gave birth to a child from rape said, "They took it away,
washed it, and I never saw it." Another said, "if anyone had tried to
show it to me after it was born, I'd have strangled them and the baby
too."[66] While one woman described herself as being on the brink of
madness while she was pregnant, others committed suicide. The
woman is faced with the terrible dilemma that her own child is also
the enemy's child, a mixture of both her own body and the evil that
has invaded her. This split between one's self and the enemy within
remains a constant pain for the woman who decides to rear the child,
since the child's physical resemblance to the father–rapist is a constant
reminder of the mother's torture. In these situations, the clash between love and hatred, acceptance and rejection mark the relation
between mother and child, and the child's life becomes extremely
traumatic as well.[67] In all of these instances, the objectification and

attendant humiliation that the women underwent in sexual torture becomes replicated in their relation to their own bodies and their relation to the world. These feelings are exacerbated when pregnancy follows rape, and even more so when pregnancy leads to childbirth.

The experience of forced impregnation can be linked to the phenomenon of abjection discussed by Julia Kristeva in *Powers of Horror*. Confronted with this thing in her belly, the woman sees it as opposed to her self, her "I." Yet this foreign thing in her belly is also part of her. She does not assimilate it; yet in expelling it she is also expelling herself. The thing in her belly is at the borderline of systems; it is ambiguous and thus disturbs the possibility of an ordered system for the structure of the self. The thing in her belly is not only disturbing the boundary between her self and the other but it also disturbs the boundaries between friend and enemy, between inside and outside, since through the pregnancy the external enemy has become the enemy within. This violation of the borders of her self may cause the feeling of abjection, a complex feeling of loathing and abhorrence of that which is beyond the possible, tolerable, and thinkable. The analysis of institutional oppression I present below supports Kristeva's claim that this abjection is also the underside of religious, moral, and ideological codes.[68]

The moral phenomenology of oppression and violence focuses on the subjective distortions of moral relations. These distortions, however, arise in a distinctive institutional, historical, and symbolic context. I will mention briefly some of the institutional factors that created a climate of patriarchal violence. First of all, one must consider the ways in which the stylization of masculinity in the military is conducive to misogyny and an inclination to rape. Some years ago in Jutland, Denmark, during a NATO exercise, soldiers were shouting a drill song, "Rape! Burn! Kill!" which the officers explained "was only for fun."[69] One military sociologist writes that the shaping of masculinity in the military "does not mean that every soldier rapes. But it does mean that the construction of the soldier—or to express it differently, the subjective identity that armies make available, by fusing certain cultural ideas of masculinity with a soldier's essence—is more conducive to certain ways of behavior rather than others."[70]

Second, one must consider the role of political propaganda. For example, in 1992 a document called "Warning" signed by the Serbian ruling party, the Serbian Socialist Party, the Serbian Academy of Arts and Sciences, and the Serbian Orthodox Church included the claim that "Albanians, Muslims, and Romans [sic], with their high birth rates, are beyond rational and human reproduction." The document called for stimulating the birth rate in some areas while suppressing it in others.[71] This political rhetoric was used to instill fear of a demographic threat to the Serbian nation and inflame nationalist sentiment among the Serbs.

Third, one must consider the role of religious institutions in contributing to nationalist, misogynist, and militarist sentiment. In 1994 the leader of the Serbian Orthodox Church delivered a Christmas message that called for Serbian women to bear more children. He proclaimed that women who do not procreate sin against themselves, against the Serbian nation, and against God Himself. Women who do not bear many children "today bitterly cry and pull their hair in despair over the loss of the only son in war." This attitude is reflected in the aphorism that "for every Serbian soldier dead in battle in Slovenia, Serbian mothers must bear 100 more fighters!"[72]

Fourth, one must consider the role of educational institutions, which are controlled agents of socialization. A study of the elementary school textbooks published in the Serbian language in 1992 shows the existence of clear patriarchal patterns: in the textbook narratives, girls were characterized by responsibility, servility, and charity, while boys were characterized by courage, intellectual curiosity, and adventurousness. The textbooks also incorporated material representing war in a positive manner. Thus, the creation of readiness for war and heroic deeds seems to be part of a systematic effort. These texts also define women's relation to war as the mothers or wives of those who wage war or the victims of war disasters. A corollary to this elementary educational material is the disproportion between male and female university graduates, with lifelong consequences for women's employment opportunities, economic independence, and social power.[73] All of these institutional factors—a militarized masculinity, patriarchal forms of nationalism and religion, inequality and bias in women's educational and employment opportunities—are inseparably linked, as Virginia Woolf already tellingly analyzed in her 1938 work *Three Guineas*. It is these factors that connect the tyrannies and servilities of the public and private worlds and that must be challenged to prevent wars.[74]

In addition to the corporal and institutional violence discussed above, war rape and sexual torture are part of a system of representational violence.[75] Symbolic pairs that recur in the war discourses include mother and nation, victim and aggressor, sexuality and death, pure and impure. In all of these pairs one can discern the unstable logic that Beauvoir illustrated in her discussion of symbolic representations. These dualisms illustrate a dynamic of ambivalence, where one term is sometimes identical, sometimes in opposition to its paired term and where woman becomes the mediating link that can sustain these fluctuating meanings.[76]

The identification of the mother's body with the earth and the territory of the nation is a deeply rooted symbolic coupling in many cultures, with one example given by the Cheyenne Indian saying: "A nation is not conquered until the women's hearts lay on the ground. Only then is this nation finished. This regardless of how brave its men are or how strong its weapons are."[77] The nation takes the image of great motherhood to represent itself, which leads to equating the rape of women with the rape of the territory, as in the Rape of Nanking. This symbolic identification is typically used for ideological and political purposes to encourage reproduction. Thus, this discourse maintains the association of woman with her capacity as a reproductive vessel. On the other hand, this coupling between motherhood and the nation is not consistently maintained. When motherhood is connected with women of flesh and blood who have been violated, the women are mostly left nameless and regarded as irrelevant by this nationalist discourse. Indeed, lingering on the fate of particular victims may be viewed as endangering the sustenance of nationalistic loyalties.

Women also symbolically become the mediating link between the image of victim and of aggressor. Thus, the woman as victim becomes a public part of this discourse, which fits well with the social role of women in public. If the mother is victimized, then the nation must be the pure victim as well, and its enemy must be the pure aggressor. This logic is used to justify aggressive military strategies, purportedly to protect the nation's women. This logic ultimately relies on the instability of the dichotomy between victim and aggressor: by virtue of its identity as victim, the nation can become the aggressor without losing its status as threatened victim. The identification of women with the image of the victim creates what some researchers have called the Rape Victim Identity, which not only brings the plight of Muslim and Croatian women to the forefront to the exclusion of Serbian women but also reiterates the image of the weak, voiceless woman whose body rather than whose words communicate her fate.[78]

Woman also becomes the mediating image in representations of sexuality and death. In peaceful times, woman's body is portrayed as the erotic object of male sexual desire, as evidenced in advertising and pornography. In wartime, her body also becomes projected as the receptacle for feelings toward death, which in some men might be expressed as necrophilia. Thus, the picture of the violated and dead woman replaces the picture of the idolized woman. The representation of death through the image of the dead body of a woman is not a new achievement of wartime. Writing about the representation of dead women in Western culture, Elisabeth Bronfen notes, "The feminine corpse inspires the surviving man to write, to deny or to acknowledge death, while at the same time the corpse is the site at which he can articulate this knowledge."[79] The symbolic opposition between sexuality and death turns into the literal identification of the two when erotic desire becomes perverted and is connected with aggressive military dominance. Thus, on the symbolic level an eroticization of violence takes place that is not always present on the phenomenological level.

In all of these ambivalent pairs—mother/nation, victim/aggressor, sexuality/death—it is the pure woman who is idolized and the polluted woman who is hated. Bosnian Muslims frequently cite the story of Emina, a young Muslim woman who sought to defend her village against the Serbian Chetniks in World War II. Unable to hold them off, she said, "Only leave me my honor; I will forgive you my death." And in 1980, Pope John Paul II used the image of a young woman who had died resisting rape as an image of female purity. Yet although a woman's purity is to be preserved, she is the first to be accused if it is lost. If a woman accuses a man of rape in Islamic culture, her case is judged before a religious court that requires four respectable Muslim witnesses to the rape to render a guilty verdict against the perpetrator.[80] And, as polluted, a woman is worthless—hence, the reaction of the Muslim father who gave his raped daughter a rope to hang herself, the reaction of husbands who divorced their raped wives, and women's fear that their rape would be discovered by their husbands. Honor and purity thus became an item of symbolic barter during wartime violence. A perpetrator would claim, "it is an honor to belong to me," and bearing his child would purify the woman of the pollution of her ethnic identity. Yet this "honor" is felt as defiling by the woman and viewed as a dishonor by her own community.

Ethics and Repair

I have tried to illustrate Beauvoir's insight that ethical reflection must consider the violations of human freedom that occur on the phenomenological, institutional, and symbolic levels and to show that this approach makes a crucial methodological contribution to feminist ethics. The work of repair in ethics must consist of interventions on these three levels. In the remainder of this chapter, I will raise the following questions: Is "recognition" the appropriate model for ethical repair on both individual and collective levels? If not, what alternatives to this paradigm are available? Although some feminist theorists argue for a modification of the notion of recognition for feminist ethics, others argue that it should be replaced as a paradigm altogether. In particular, I will discuss the proposals that ethical relations are better understood through the concepts of "witnessing"[81] or of an "ethics of alterity."[82]

The term "recognition" is well entrenched in both philosophical and everyday vocabularies. Its connotations are (a) epistemological, (b) existential, and (c) political. The epistemological connotation of recognition involves knowing that something is true, as in the claim that the perspective of feminist or race theory is true. The existential connotation of the term implies an affirmation of the validity of one's identity. Recognition in the existential sense is thus opposed to the misrecognition of racist or ethnic prejudice, which distorts and damages persons or groups through demeaning pictures of themselves. The political meaning of recognition invokes acknowledgment of different groups as equals in the political arena, as occurs in debates about multiculturalism.[83] One of the central features of the concept of recognition is the view that human life is fundamentally *intersubjective* and *dialogic*. Recognition calls into question the Kantian approach to moral reasoning, which approaches morality first through the individual's relation to the moral law and takes account of others through additional moral virtues such as "empathy" or an "enlarged mentality." Hegel's analysis of the dialectic of recognition, in which the self is constituted though his or her relation to the other, has become paradigmatic for this notion. In the *Phenomenology of Spirit* he writes that the master and slave consciousnesses "recognized themselves as mutually recognizing one another."[84]

In considering what kind of ethical repair is needed for one who has suffered the humiliation and degradation of sexual violence in war, intersubjective and dialogic relations are crucial. Through establishing safe intimate relations and public forums in which individuals can risk speaking about traumatic violations, individuals and communities can begin to recover. Psychological studies of trauma, like Judith Lewis Herman's exemplary *Trauma and Recovery*, show how such recovery may take place through establishing safe relationships between victims and family members, friends, and support groups. Notably, the intersubjective interaction in which an individual narrates the trauma is not a confrontation between victim and persecutor—although the dream of having one's day in court may lead to staging that confrontation. The philosopher Susan Brison also emphasizes the necessity of narrating one's trauma to empathic others to rebuild one's trust in the world and to acknowledge that one's autonomy is dependent on others.[85] In this respect, the focus on intersubjectivity in an ethics of recovery steers away from one of the central features of Hegel's discussion of recognition, namely, that recognition occurs through a dialectical relation between *antagonistic* forms of consciousness.

One feminist philosopher who argues for the significance of recognition in moral and political philosophy is Seyla Benhabib. For Benhabib, confrontation with the concrete other, as she calls it, is "a 'struggle for recognition' in the Hegelian sense" and is necessary to hear the voice of the other.[86] Without this concrete confrontation, one commits one of two errors. (1) One addresses only the "generalized other," i.e., the rational features that make the other like me, and not the concrete other in her or his difference from me. But in this strategy, the other as different from myself disappears and it becomes incoherent to talk about "universalizability." (2) One addresses the concrete other, but only through a projection of one's own fantasy or feelings. Feelings of empathy risk being merely such projections and effectively ignore the concrete differences of the other. For Benhabib, the only way of acknowledging concrete differences is through the Hegelian notion that difference appears through struggle. Benhabib also emphasizes the notion of reciprocity that is implicit in Hegel's concept of recognition. I am an "other" to you, and you are an "I" to yourself but an "other" to me. It is because of the reciprocity in intersubjective relations that one can reverse perspectives, listen, and understand the other, and thereby carry out a moral conversation with a concrete other, as well as entertain the hope that one can extend this conversation to all of humanity. Benhabib invokes this notion of reversibility of perspectives to think from the standpoint of all involved and ask, "What would it really be like to reason from the standpoint of a black welfare mother?"[87] Benhabib connects this ability to think from the perspective of everyone else with Hannah Arendt's notion of enlarged mentality. When these actual conversations cannot take place, such a dialogue can be imagined or simulated.

Does Benhabib's conception of recognition and reversibility of perspectives illuminate intersubjective engagement if the paradigm instance is the relation between perpetrator and victim rather than master and slave?[88] The notion of reciprocal recognition does diagnose one way that moral relations break down. Because of the perpetrator's dehumanization and humiliation of the victim, he does not acknowledge the concrete identity of the other, and recognition cannot be taken as a description of this intersubjective dynamic. But the concept of recognition still might have validity as a normative ideal, in providing a call for recognition of the concrete identity of other. Only when a perpetrator can begin to think of the women he raped and murdered as particular persons, not just as "tall, dark-haired, and between twenty and twenty-five years of age," is there some hope for moral contact. When the perpetrator is able to think how his sister would feel if someone did to her what he is about to do to another young woman, then a certain listening takes place, and a moral relation can be established. But as a normative ideal, Benhabib's notion of reversibility would imply that a victim should also consider, what would it really be like to reason from the standpoint of a Serbian/Muslim/Croatian man who rapes and tortures? Such an expectation would show no moral consideration for the victim of violence. Nor would the victim's attempt to understand the standpoint of her rapist bring about the conditions for moral relations between them. The only way to establish moral dialogue might be the challenge of the young woman to her aggressor: Imagine your sister in my position. Thus, there is a hidden premise in Benhabib's notion of reversibility: reversibility is a norm with emancipatory intent that calls on those with power to reason from the position of those without power.

It is the asymmetry of relations, particularly between those with different social positions, that leads Iris Marion Young to challenge Benhabib's call to imaginatively adopt the perspective of another. Young argues that Benhabib's interpretation of enlarged mentality obscures the difference and particularity of the other, even though it is precisely these features that Benhabib seeks to acknowledge in moral relations. Young argues that differences cannot be imaginatively overcome, and the attempt to do so merely results in the projection of one's own fantasies onto others. Like Benhabib, Young supports the Hegelian principle of reciprocal recognition. But unlike her, she argues that reciprocal recognition cannot be achieved through reversibility of standpoints. Standpoints are themselves constituted by the asymmetrical relations between self and other, as in the generational asymmetry between mother and daughter, or the positional asymmetry between black and white men. Hence, reciprocal recognition can be achieved only through understanding the relation between self and other as asymmetrical and irreversible. Thus, according to Young, the principle of reversibility fails to explain moral communication from either the standpoint of the privileged or the standpoint of the oppressed. For the person who is privileged, reversibility of perspectives would entail imaginatively projecting one's fears and fantasies onto the other, e.g., fear of being paralyzed or blinded. Asking the one who is oppressed "to

reverse perspectives with the privileged in adjudicating a conflict may
itself be an injustice and an insult."[89] Instead, reciprocal recognition
can best be gained by cultivating the virtue of moral humility, a "hum-
ble recognition" that one cannot put oneself in another's position but
can learn significantly through listening to the other person. The example of the soldier who was able to listen to his victim and think how
he would feel if an aggressor attacked his sister, according to Young's
analysis, would be an illustration of the asymmetry between the perspectives of victim and perpetrator. The Serbian soldier could learn
from this young Muslim woman not because he was able to put himself
in her position but because he understood the difference between them
as similar to another difference that he could respond to, namely, that
between himself and his sister.

Thus, Young's focus on asymmetry makes an important contribution to the concept of reciprocal recognition, which implies that
"each standpoint is constituted by internal relations to other standpoints."[90] Since relations between standpoints may shift according to
developments in contexts, these perspectives cannot be treated as
fixed or rigid. In the example of sexual violence during civil war, the
differences that turned neighbors into enemies became radical differences through political propaganda and the fact of violence. Therefore, the moral humility that Young proposes must include, as she
implicitly acknowledges, an understanding of the collective social
processes that transform social differences into fixed categories. Enlarged mentality, in Young's interpretation of Hannah Arendt's concept, must include an understanding of this web of social relations and
the plurality of perspectives.

Young is more explicit than Benhabib that certain perspectives
should be given moral priority, such as the perspectives of the oppressed,
and in this regard she echoes a kind of standpoint theory. Yet she does
not deny that "even under the conditions of injustice, the interests and
perspectives of those who belong to privileged groups should not be dis-
regarded."[91] However, she does not make clear how the perspectives of
the privileged are to be taken into account. Moreover, Young still maintains a dyadic model in which asymmetrical reciprocal recognition takes
place between two opposing forms of consciousness. But in the relation
between persecutor and victim, the persecutor cannot expect that his

perspective will either be legitimated or forgiven by the victim. Nor can the victim expect recognition as a concrete person from the persecutor, though in some cases this does occur.[92] The victim's claim for epistemological, existential, and political affirmation must be satisfied through other relations. The need for affirmation cannot be fulfilled through a triadic model either, positing a third person who recognizes the perspective of the victim. As Herman's research indicates, for a victim to heal her wounds after trauma, she must establish safe relations with people who themselves have relations that help them bear the burden of trauma. One of the ethical implications of this psychological research is that the condition for ethical repair and recovery from past traumas is an interlocking network of relations among a plurality of subjectivities. The nature of the public narrative set in process by these linked relations is crucial for the possibility of affirming the truth of victims' experiences, identities, and political rights.[93]

Thus, feminist philosophers who have worked with the model of recognition have introduced a number of modifications to the standard account. Both Benhabib and Young move away from the physical and metaphysical oppositions present in Hegel's discussion of the life-and-death struggle between master and slave. In their interpretation, recognition becomes recognition of the social constitution of subjectivity, of the social differences among embodied subjectivities, and of the normative demand to listen to the perspective of the concrete other. They differ, though, on whether understanding one another across difference and understanding collective social processes are best described by a process of reciprocal recognition that is reversible or irreversible.

Other feminists are more skeptical about the usefulness of Hegel's notion of reciprocal recognition for ethics. Cynthia Willet challenges the Hegelian model of the master–slave dialectic by arguing that it works with a model of identity that seeks to subordinate differences within a larger identity. In her reading, the Hegelian dialectic of recognition presumes that the individual recognize the other as similar to oneself. Instead, she argues that the dynamics of mutual recognition are better understood through the face-to-face play between parent and infant. Affect attunement, not antagonism, is thus the basis of social reciprocity. The sensual roots of recognition in maternal–infant relations not only provide an alternative to a Hegelian model, according to Willet, but also historically have provided resources for resistance in the face of oppression.[94]

Kelly Oliver seeks to reject, or more precisely reconstruct, the term "recognition," because of its implicit presupposition of an essential antagonism between subjects. Oliver is concerned with the question of how to repair subjectivities that have been destroyed by torture or enslavement. To this end, she proposes the notion of witnessing, a nonantagonistic model of intersubjectivity that includes the addressability of the subject who can speak of trauma and the responseability of the one who is addressed. Together, these moments constitute the process of witnessing that, according to Oliver, should be taken as the paradigm for subjectivity. Witnessing bears the double meaning of eyewitness testimony, which refers to the subject's position as spectator to an event, and bearing witness, which refers to the response-ability of subjectivity that goes beyond eyewitness testimony. Oliver argues that only the model of witnessing, and not an antagonistic model of recognition, can "support the normative force of ethical obligations to be responsible to others rather than exclude or kill them."[95]

Oliver makes two contributions to theorizing about ethical subjectivity. First, in moving away from an antagonistic model of intersubjectivity, she addresses the conditions of ethical healing following trauma. It is not antagonistic relations that provide the source of recovery for a victim of trauma or rape but the relations that are safely outside this fundamental antagonism. Second, she moves away from a paradigm of subjectivity that presumes that oppression and traumatization are fundamentally constitutive of subjectivity, a paradigm that she finds in the works of Judith Butler. Instead of viewing subjectivity as constituted by a fundamental ontological trauma, one should examine the specific institutional and social forms of oppression and violence that damage subjectivity.

Oliver follows Luce Irigaray in arguing that we need to move "beyond recognition" in order to think the "recognition of difference."[96] She proposes a notion of subjective relations based on a model of the loving look that involves all the senses and that moves away from the model of the objectifying look, which still thinks subjectivity in terms of subjects and objects. Citing Irigaray, as well as black feminist writers like bell hooks and Patricia Williams who are inspired by Martin Luther King's proclamation, "I have decided to love," she proposes a love ethics that stresses the primacy of connection instead of alienation. For Oliver, the ability to address and respond in intersubjective relations is a testimony of love, which affirms our relation to the world and to other people.

Does Oliver's notion of the loving look adequately attend to the ethical needs of a subject who seeks to recover from traumatic events? On the one hand, Oliver does point to the need for multiple nonantagonistic relations involved in ethical repair, and from this perspective her attempt to shift away from an antagonist paradigm is fruitful. On the other hand, her move to an ethics of love is accompanied by a utopianism that overlooks the fundamental role of ambivalence and conflict in loving relations. Conflicts, disagreements, and ambivalence, whereby both hatred and love are simultaneously directed toward the same person, are part of the intersubjective dynamics of all love relations.[97] Like Irigaray, she underplays this conflictual and ambivalent dimension of the very human relations that she takes as her model for witnessing. Even in the supportive, nonantagonistic relation between patient and therapist, the therapist needs to set sharp boundaries so as to avoid the complete invasion of her emotional life by the patient's trauma. At other times, the therapist finds herself identifying with the patient to such an extent that she feels that her professional skills become jeopardized. In intimate relations as well, the very loving relation that ought to be a source of recovery from trauma may become a repetition of the trauma, as in the example of the woman survivor of war rape who replicated sadistic–masochistic behavior in her new marriage.

Moreover, in addressing recovery or repair from traumatic experiences on a societal level, the notion of the loving look is not adequate to deal with the complexity of the process of recovery. Societies seeking ethical repair—e.g., in the former Yugoslavia, in postapartheid South Africa—need to address the fact that some of its members were perpetrators and some victims. Not only would it be unrealistic but also morally disrespectful of victims to view the task of reconciliation as a transformation of the totalizing antagonisms that were constructed through wartime propaganda and violence into relations of love. More plausibly, reconciliation would enable those who have suffered violence to publicly affirm the truth of their experiences, the validity of their identities, and their claim for equal political rights. These tasks—which are commonly associated with the concept of recognition—presuppose neither an ontological antagonism between subjects nor a love that transcends conflict. But they do presuppose the view that, though human relations are not necessarily structured by relations of *domination*, human *conflict* persists in multiple and changeable forms. Hence, there is a need for public forums for judging and mediating conflicts. Witnessing can be considered one of the achievements of such public forums. The person who testifies to traumatic experiences can be said, as Oliver argues, to reconstitute an inner witness even as the testimony is addressed to an external witness.[98]

The concept of witnessing must also face the issue of false witnessing. A form of false witnessing was keenly present during the work of the Truth and Reconciliation Commission in South Africa. Since all who testified were offered amnesty for their crimes, many police officers ensured they kept their jobs and pensions by participating in the formal ritual of testifying, while showing arrogant contempt for the proceedings.

False witnessing also takes place when not all who are present at a testimony become witnesses in the sense of accepting the moral task of listening. Oliver does speak to the issue of false witnessing, which she describes as a result of closing off, of refusing to work through one's blind spots or to attend to the power differential between subject positions, and refusing to value differences. But this analysis of false witnessing does not provide the tools for healing for the victims. As Beauvoir argued, in ethics one must address the risk of failure—in this case the failure of witnessing. Since false witnessing does in fact occur, can witnessing provide an adequate model for recovery from trauma? In some situations, victims' testimony does establish the public forum as a witness to their traumas in a way that affirms the truth of the victims' experiences, the validity of their identities, and their claim for equal rights. But this approach needs to be complemented by other strategies, which may include punishment for the perpetrator, restitution to victims and their families, and affirmative measures to establish social and economic equality. The concept of witnessing does provide an emotional depth to the process of listening across differences. But in claiming that witnessing, as response-ability and address-ability, is the basis of all subjectivity, Oliver overlooks the element of conflict within the process of witnessing. Moreover, she marginalizes the institutional and symbolic constituents of embodied ethical subjectivity that are crucial both for the fact of trauma and for subsequent efforts of ethical recovery and repair.

In contrast to Oliver, Ewa Ziarek in her book *An Ethics of Dissensus* maintains a focus on the antagonistic dimension of "discourse, embodiment and democratic politics."[99] She underscores that there is an ineradicable aspect of conflict within individual subjectivity, as well as between subjects in struggles against domination, injustice, and inequalities. Her term "dissensus," from the Latin *dissensio*, meaning disagreement and struggle, indicates that the work of ethics is not based on achieving consensus, as Benhabib would argue, but on negotiating irreducible conflicts. The term "dissensus" is also meant to highlight the root *sensus*, pointing to the sensuous dimension of ethical relations. Thus, dissensus refers both to the failure of formal linguistic consent and the material conflicts rooted in sexual drives and social relations. Ziarek's project is to work through an ethics that is based on respect for and responsibility toward the Other, what she calls an ethics of alterity. Like Oliver, she draws on the work of the French philosopher Emmanuel Levinas, who argues that responsibility to the Other is prior to individual intentionality or will. For Levinas, the primary moment of subjectivity is the exposure to the Other, so that the Other is in one's skin.[100] Otherness is not the negative or opposite against which the identity of a subject or a community is constituted. Viewing the Other as an adversary perpetuates the notion that the Other is the site of our alienation and, hence, the object of our ambivalence and hatred.[101] Instead, the Other in Levinas's and Ziarek's view has a singularity toward which one bears responsibility. Ziarek differs from Oliver, however, in emphasizing the irreducible element of conflict in ethics. In referring to the work of the black American writer bell hooks, Ziarek notes that one cannot separate love from rage, or ethical obligation from the existence of antagonisms.[102] Conflicts exist both within individual subjects, what

Julia Kristeva calls the internal alterity within the subject, and in intersubjective relations.

Although Ziarek seeks to show that there are multiple levels of conflict that ethics must negotiate, her term "dissensus" is still linked by opposition to the term "consensus," which gives priority to the discursive dimension of ethical negotiation. One might well choose the more commonplace term "conflict" instead, to refer to the multiple dimensions of conflict that exist on phenomenological, institutional, and symbolic levels. In contrast to the widely used phrase among feminist philosophers, an "ethics of care," an ethics of conflict underscores that even relations of love and care are not free from destructiveness and ambivalence. Moreover, the phrase "ethics of conflict" includes the connotation of the institutional clashes that are involved in wartime violence, as well as the symbolic contradictions that maintain ideologies of domination. An ethics of conflict points to the irremediable dimension of failure within ethics, which cannot be put aside even while one engages in the constructive and creative future-oriented visions of repair and social transformation. Because the conflicts that create ethical failure occur on subjective, institutional, and symbolic levels, a language of witnessing that addresses a face-to-face encounter is not sufficient.

In referring to the work of repair in ethics, Ziarek uses phrases like "recognition and respect for the alterity of the Other" and "just judgment."[103] She invokes these terms to show that postmodern discourse does indeed have a normative dimension. Given the irreducible element of conflict in ethical relations, one must ask how these terms are meaningfully thought in the face of their failure. What effects can the concepts of respect for alterity and just judgments have when they are patently lacking in practice, as in cases of active or passive participation in inflicting physical or psychological violence? These terms are useful for the educative work necessary to invigorate the future of democracy. But they are less useful for facing the present transgression of ethical relations. The concept of responsibility, also invoked by both Ziarek and Oliver, is more useful for addressing the paradigm case of violence. In recovery from violence, the victim needs to place responsibility for transgression outside herself, and she is enabled in this task by the interlocking links of human relations. The perpetrator is faced with the demand to acknowledge responsibility; sometimes this demand is successful, sometimes unsuccessful. It is this call to assign responsibility that resonates in black American theorists of race relations such as Patricia Williams and bell hooks, who demand accountability for racist, sexist, and economic oppression.[104] But even when responsibility for wrongdoing is not acknowledged by the perpetrator, responsibility can still be assigned. But neither the victim nor public can assign respect for alterity to a perpetrator. Hence, for the philosopher Hannah Arendt, who wrote about Eichmann's trial in Jerusalem, the crucial dimension of ethics in the contemporary world is that responsibility exists even though it is disassociated from subjective intentions. As Arendt noted, in contemporary evil, individuals' intentions rarely correspond to the magnitude of evil that individuals can cause.[105] Hence, responsibility exists even when victims' demands for epistemological, existential, and political recognition are frustrated by the perpetrators.

In this chapter, I have tried to show that ethics must take the concepts of failure and conflict as central, as Beauvoir suggests, in order to address the persistent realities of conflict in human affairs. Moreover, I have tried to show that ethics includes phenomenological, institutional, and symbolic dimensions, even though this approach may be viewed as trespassing boundaries between ethical and political analysis. This project is specifically feminist in taking its inspiration from an analysis of sexual atrocities that philosophers have typically ignored in their ethical reflections. But the implications of an ethics of conflict are not limited to addressing issues of sexual violence. Rather, it suggests a strategy that is productive for ethical analyses of oppression and violence more generally. The concepts of asymmetrical recognition and witnessing are important for addressing one dimension of ethical repair, but they are not definitive of ethical subjectivity or ethical repair. Responsibility, not merely in terms of the subjective ability to respond but in terms of an intersubjective and public judgment of responsibility, is decisive for both individual and collective ethical repair.

Notes

1. Immanuel Kant, "Religion within the boundaries of mere reason," in *Religion and Rational Theology*, trans. and ed. Allen W. Wood and George Di Giovanni (Cambridge: Cambridge University Press, 1996), 69.

2. Jean Vickers, *Women and War* (London: Zed Books Ltd., 1993), 2.

3. For literature on these issues in feminist ethics, see, for example: Bat-Ami Bar On and Ann Ferguson, eds., *Daring To Be Good: Essays in Feminist Ethico-Politics*, (New York: Routledge, 1998); Claudia Card, ed., *Feminist Ethics* (Lawrence: University Press of Kansas, 1991) and *On Feminist Ethics and Politics* (Lawrence: University Press of Kansas, 1999); Eve Browning Cole and Susan Coultrap-McQuin, eds., *Explorations in Feminist Ethics: Theory and Practice* (Bloomington: Indiana University Press, 1992); Chris Cuomo, *Feminism and Ecological Communities: An Ethics of Flourishing* (New York: Routledge, 1998); Peggy Des Autels and Joanne Waugh, eds., *Feminists Doing Ethics* (Lanham, Md.: Rowman & Littlefield, 2001); Miranda Fricker and Jennifer Hornsby, eds., *The Cambridge Companion to Feminism in Philosophy* (Cambridge: Cambridge University Press, 2000); Carol Gilligan, *In a Different Voice: Psychological Theory and Women's Development* (Cambridge, Mass.: Harvard University Press, 1982); Susan J. Hekman, *Moral Voices Moral Selves: Carol Gilligan and Feminist Moral Theory* (Cambridge: Polity Press, 1995); Virginia Held, *Feminist Morality: Transforming Culture, Society, and Politics* (Chicago: University of Chicago Press, 1993); Eva Feder Kittay and Diana T. Meyers, eds., *Women and Moral Theory* (Totawa, N.J.: Rowman & Littlefield, 1987); Eva Feder Kittay, *Love's Labor: Essays on Women, Equality and Dependency* (New York: Routledge, 1999); Luce Irigaray, *An Ethics of Sexual Difference*, trans. Carolyn Burke and Gillian C. Gill (London: Athlone Press, 1993); Diana Tietjens Meyers, ed., *Feminists Rethink the Self* (Boulder, Colo.: Westview Press, 1997); Catriona Mackenzie and Natalie Stoljar, eds., *Relational Autonomy: Feminist Perspectives on Autonomy, Agency, and the Social Self* (Oxford: Oxford University Press, 2000); Sara Ruddick, *Maternal Thinking: Towards a Politics of Peace* (Boston: Beacon Press, 1989); Laurie Shrage, *Moral Dilemmas of Feminism: Prostitution, Adultery and Abortion* (New York: Routledge, 1994); Rosemarie Tong, *Feminine and Feminist Ethics* (Belmont, Calif.: Wadsworth, 1993); Joan C. Tronto, *Moral Boundaries: A Political Argument for an Ethic of Care* (New York: Routledge, 1994).

4. Margaret Urban Walker, *Moral Understandings: A Feminist Study in Ethics* (New York: Routledge, 1998), 5. My discussion here draws on her approach to morality, which she names the expressive-collaborative model, 3–28.

5. In *Eichmann in Jerusalem*, Hannah Arendt notes that during the trial Eichmann declared that "he had lived his whole life according to Kant's moral precepts." Apparently, though, he had followed the distorted categorical imperative of the Third Reich: "Act in such a way that the Führer,

if he knew your action, would approve it" ([New York: Penguin, 1992] 135–36).

6. The phrase "gray zone" was used by the Italian scientist, Jew, and concentration camp survivor Primo Levi in his book *The Drowned and the Saved* (New York: Vintage, 1989), 42, and is discussed by Claudia Card in "Groping through Gray Zones," in *On Feminist Ethics and Politics*, 3–26.

7. Susan Neimann, "Theodocy in Jerusalem," in *Hannah Arendt in Jerusalem*, ed. Steven E. Ascheim (Berkeley: University of California Press, 2001).

8. George Alfred Schrader, Jr., "The Status of Value," photocopy, 2.

9. Schrader, "Normative and Descriptive Meaning in Ethics," photocopy, 9–11.

10. Walker, *Moral Understandings*, 15.

11. Walker, *Moral Understandings*, 22.

12. Walker, *Moral Understandings*, 52. Walker terms this approach to ethics the theoretical-juridical model. She proposes as an alternative the expressive-collaborative model, "which looks at moral life as a continuing negotiation *among* people. . . . As a philosophical model, this representation of morality functions both descriptively and normatively. Descriptively, it aims to reveal what morality "is"—what kinds of interactions go on that can be recognized as moral ones. Normatively, it aims to suggest some important things morality is "for"—what in human lives depends on there being such practices, and how these practices can go better or worse" (p. 60). This model underscores that guiding decisions is but one role of morality. Morality also helps us explain who we and others are, to whom we are accountable, how wrongs can be repaired, and how to understand our own moral feelings (p. 62).

13. Linda A. Bell, *Rethinking Ethics in the Midst of Violence* (Lanham, Md.: Rowman & Littlefield, 1993), 25.

14. See Debra Bergoffen, "February 22, 2001: Toward a Politics of the Vulnerable Body," in *Hypatia, Special Issue: Feminist Philosophy and the Problem of Evil*, ed. Robin May Schott (Bloomington: Indiana University Press, Winter 2003).

15. Ewa Ziarek, *The Ethics of Dissensus* (Stanford, Calif.: Stanford University Press, 2001), 2.

16. My discussion of Beauvoir is drawn from my article "Beauvoir on the Ambiguity of Evil," in *Cambridge Companion to the Philosophy of Simone de Beauvoir*, ed. Claudia Card (Cambridge: Cambridge University Press, 2003).

17. Beauvoir, *Ethics*, 34.

18. See, for example, Catriona Mackenzie and Natalie Stoljar, eds., *Relational Autonomy: Feminist Perspectives on Autonomy, Agency and the Social Self* (Oxford: Oxford University Press, 2000) and Diana Tietjens Meyers, ed., *Feminists Rethink the Self* (Boulder, Colo.: Westview Press, 1997).

19. Beauvoir, *Ethics*, 72.

20. Beauvoir, *The Second Sex*, 158.

21. Beauvoir, *Ethics*, 98.

22. See Margaret A. Simons, *Beauvoir and the Second Sex: Feminism, Race, and the Origins of Existentialism* (Lanham, Md.: Rowman & Littlefield, 1999). Especially relevant here is chapter 11, "Richard Wright, Simone de Beauvoir, and the Second Sex," 167–84. Simons also problematizes the way in which Beauvoir separates racism and sexism as distinct, though analogous, categories.

23. Simons, *Beauvoir*, 152.

24. Beauvoir, *America Day by Day*, trans. Carol Cosman (London: Phoenix, 1999), 243. Sartre gives a similar analysis of anti-Semites in *Anti-Semite and Jew*.

25. Beauvoir, *America*, 237.

26. Beauvoir, *America*, 89.

27. Virginia Held, *Feminist Morality: Transforming Culture, Society and Politics* (Chicago: University of Chicago Press, 1993). See, for example, chapter one, "The Feminist Transformation of Consciousness and Culture," 1–21. Diana Tietjens Meyers also focuses on how moral concepts are conveyed through cultural messages of inferiority and superiority. Meyers, "Emotion and Heterodox Moral Perception: An Essay in Moral Social Psychology," in *Feminists Rethink the Self*, ed. Diana Tietjens Meyers, 197–218. The political theorist Drucilla Cornell also focuses on the role of the imaginary and the symbolic for ethical transformation in *Beyond Accommodation: Ethical Feminism, Deconstruction and the Law* (New York: Routledge, 1991) and *Transformations* (New York: Routledge, 1993).

28. Beauvoir, *The Second Sex*, xx.

29. Beauvoir, *The Second Sex*, 90, 223.

30. Beauvoir, *The Second Sex*, 217.

31. Penelope Deutscher argues in *Yielding Gender* that it is precisely through its contradictions that a patriarchal discourse is able to maintain itself.

32. Antony Beevor, *Berlin: The Downfall, 1945* (New York: Viking, 2002).

33. E.g., this controversy is referred to by Renata Jambresic Kirin in "Personal Narratives on War: A Challenge to Women's Essays and Ethnography in Croatia," in *War Discourse, Women's Discourse*, ed. Svetlana Slapsak (Ljubljana, Slovenia: Topos, 2000), 295.

34. This phrase is invoked by Beverly Allen in *Rape Warfare: The Hidden Genocide in Bosnia-Herzegovina and Croatia* (Minneapolis: University of Minnesota Press, 1996), 106.

35. Allen, *Rape*, 86.

36. Mirsad Tokaca, ed., *The Sin of Silence, Risk of Speech* (Sarajevo, Mirsad Tokaca, 2000), 529. Note that the media records explosions of "domestic" violence against women, without connecting it to postwar trauma. See Biljana Kasic, "The Aestheticization of the Victim Within the Discourse of War," in Slapsak, *War Discourse*, 274.

37. Libby Tata Arcel, "Torture, cruel, inhuman and degrading treatment of women; psychological consequences" in *Torture* (Copenhagen: International Rehabilitation Council for Torture Victims, Fall 2002). In her definition, Arcel emphasizes that rape is *sexual* violence, not merely violence, since it is an attack on the embodied sexuality of the woman. It is a crime that has lifelong consequences for a woman's sexuality if the trauma is untreated. Moreover, she defines rape as a crime that has women as its primary victims, though men too can be raped. When men are victims of rape, they become feminized. Both her emphasis on the *sexual* and *gendered* nature of the crime fit well with Ann Cahill's analysis in *Rethinking Rape* (Ithaca, N.Y.: Cornell University Press, 2001).

38. Kelly Dawn Askin, *War Crimes against Women* (The Hague: Kluwer Law International), 281.

39. Arcel, "Sexual Torture of Women as a Weapon of War—The Case of Bosnia-Herzegovina," in *War Violence, Trauma and the Coping Process*, ed. Arcel (Copenhagen: International Rehabilitation Council for Torture Victims, 1998), 191.

40. Sara Ruddick, "Notes Toward a Feminist Peace Politics," in *Gendering War Talk*, ed. Miriam Cooke and Angela Woollacott (Princeton, N.J.: Princeton University Press, 1993), 110. She cites Joan Smith, "Crawling from the Wreckage," in *Misogynies* (New York: Ballantine Books, 1990) and Virginia Woolf, *Three Guineas* (New York: Harcourt Brace, 1966).

41. Todd Salzman, "'Rape Camps,' Forced Impregnation, and Ethnic Cleansing," in *War's Dirty Secret*, ed. Anne Llewellyn Barstow (Cleveland: The Pilgrim Press, 2000), 72–74. In male camps sexual assault took place as well, as in the instance of a prisoner being forced to bite off the genitals of another male prisoner.

42. Arcel, "Sexual Torture," 196.

43. Alexandra Stiglmayer, "The Rapes in Bosnia-Herzegovina," in *Mass Rape*, ed. Alexandra Stiglmayer (Lincoln: University of Nebraska, 1994), 95.

44. Stiglmayer, "Rapes," 155.

45. Stiglmayer, "Rapes," 120.

46. Askin, 282.

47. Ruth Seifert, "War and Rape: A Preliminary Analysis," in Stiglmayer, *Mass Rape*, 55.

48. Stiglmayer, "Rapes," 157–59.

49. It is not the case that unwilling perpetrators turn into willing perpetrators. The soldier cited above had fled from the Luka internment camp because he was afraid of having to kill and rape more people and thinks it would have been better had he been killed than being forced to kill others. Stiglmayer, "Rapes," 160.

50. Stiglmayer, "Rapes," 109.

51. Arcel, "Sexual Torture," 24.

52. Julia Kristeva, *Strangers to Ourselves*, trans. Leon S. Roudiez (New York: Columbia University Press, 1991), 192.

53. Arcel, "Torture," 16.

54. Here I draw in part on Libby Tata Arcel's lecture, "The Body as Language in Therapy of Sexually Tortured Women," presented at the conference "Facing Atrocities: Between Ethics and Politics," University of Copenhagen, February 28, 2002.

55. See Mary Douglas, *Purity and Danger* (London: Routledge and Kegan Paul, 1966), 4.

56. Jean Améry, *At the Mind's Limit*, trans. Sidney Rosenfeld and Stella P. Rosenfeld (London: Granta Books, 1999), 34. Améry describes torture like rape, because of the lack of consent. In torture, one's trust in the world breaks down and the person is completely transformed into flesh ("Sexual Torture," 28–33).

57. Tokaca, *Sin of Silence*, 528.

58. Arcel, "Sexual Torture," 22.

59. Douglas, *Purity and Danger*, 121.

60. Susan J. Brison, *Aftermath: Violence and the Remaking of a Self* (Princeton, N.J.: Princeton University Press, 2002), 96.

61. See Jessica Benjamin's analysis of sadomasochistic relations in "Master and Slave: The Fantasy of Erotic Domination," in *Powers of Desire: The Politics of Sexuality*, ed. Ann Snitow, Christine Stansell, and Sharon Thompson (New York: Monthly Review Press, 1983), 280–99. If one extends Benjamin's analysis, then the traumatic effects of rape reinforce the polarity between controller and controlled, violator and violated, that has its psychological origin in the splitting of impulses and assigning them respectively to men and women.

62. Arcel, "Sexual Torture," 28. Arcel refers to Judith Herman, *Trauma and Recovery* (New York: Basic Books, 1992).

63. Arcel, "Sexual Torture," 202.

64. Rhonda Copelon, "Surfacing Gender: Reconceptualizing Crimes against Women in Time of War," in *Mass Rape*, ed. Stiglmayer, 202.

65. Stiglmayer, "Rape," 119.

66. Stiglmayer, "Rape," 131–33.

67. Vesna Nicolic-Ristanovic, *Women, Violence and War* (Budapest: CEU Press, 2000), 71–72.

68. Julia Kristeva, *Powers of Horror*, trans. Leon S. Roudiez (New York: Columbia University Press, 1992), 3–4, 209.

69. Arcel, "Sexual Torture," 202.

70. Quoted in Seifert, "War and Rape," 61. For an exploration of the nature of masculinity cultivated by military institutions and practices, see Klaus Theweleit, *Male Fantasies*, Vols. 1 and 2. (Minneapolis: University of Minnesota Press, 1987, 1990). See also Cynthia Cockburn and Dubravka Yarkov, eds., *The Postwar Moment: Militaries, Masculinities and International Peacekeeping* (London: Lawrence and Wishart, 2002) for discussions of how the process of militarization, and militarizing masculinity, continues in postwar societies and in societies involved in peacekeeping missions.

71. Salzman, "Rape Camps," 65.

72. Salzman, "Rape Camps," 66.

73. Isidora Jaric, "Militaristic Values and Promotion of Patriarchal Female Roles in Elementary School Textbooks on the Territory of Serbia and Their Impact on the Social Position of Woman in Modern Yugoslav/Serbian Society," in *War Discourse*, ed. Slapsak, 257–70.

74. Virginia Woolf, *Three Guineas* (Oxford: Blackwell for Shakespeare Head Press, 2001), 130–31.

75. Biljana Kasic, "The Aesthetic of the Victim within the Discourse of War," in *War Discourse*, ed. Slapsak, 280. My discussion in this section draws on this article, 271–83.

76. In this I am following Penelope Deutscher's argument in *Yielding Gender* (London: Routledge, 1997), about the instability of the meanings of women and the feminine that sustain phallocentric concepts of reason.

77. Arcel, "Sexual Torture," 184.

78. Inger Skjelsbaek, "Sexual Violence in the Conflicts in ex-Yugoslavia," in *War Discourse*, ed. Slapsak, 134.

79. Elisabeth Bronfen, *Over Her Dead Body* (Manchester: Manchester University Press, 1992), 13. Many theorists have pointed to the connection between aggressive hostility and male eroticism. See, for example, Nancy Hartsock, *Money, Sex and Power* (New York and London: Longman, 1983), 155–85. Hartsock's perspective suggests a continuum between peace-time

and war-time eroticism. In this section, however, I am interested in the specific transmutations of eroticism through war-time representations.

80. Salzman, "Rape Camps," 81.

81. In the section on witnessing, I will discuss Kelly Oliver's suggestions in *Witnessing: Beyond Recognition* (Minneapolis: University of Minnesota Press, 2001).

82. In the final section, I will discuss Ewa Plonowska Ziarek's suggestions in *An Ethics of Dissensus* (Stanford, Calif.: Stanford University Press, 2001).

83. See, for example, Charles Taylor, "The Politics of Recognition," in *Multiculturalism*, ed. Amy Gutmann (Princeton, N.J.: Princeton University Press, 1994), 25.

84. G. W. F. Hegel, *Phenomenology of Spirit*, trans. A. V. Miller (Oxford: Oxford University Press, 1977), 112. See Beatrice Hanssen's discussion in *Critique of Violence* (London: Routledge, 2000), 190ff.

85. Susan J. Brison, *Aftermath: Violence and the Remaking of a Self* (Princeton, N.J.: Princeton University Press, 2002), 38–66.

86. Seyla Benhabib, *Situating the Self: Gender, Community and Postmodernism in Contemporary Ethics* (New York: Routledge, 1992), 168.

87. Benhabib, *Situating the Self*, 52, 168, 166.

88. It should of course be noted that many commentators have argued that Hegel's description of the dialectic between master and slave does not apply to the empirical phenomenon of slavery. For example, Cynthia Willet argues, "The duplicitous symmetries of Hegelian logic conceal, however, what African American history demonstrates: The slave was not in fact the mirror reversal of the master. The slave did not inevitably see himself or herself in terms of desires disavowed by the master." See *Maternal Ethics and Other Slave Moralities* (New York: Routledge, 1995), 106.

89. Iris Marion Young, *Intersecting Voices: Dilemmas of Gender, Political Philosophy and Policy* (Princeton, N.J.: Princeton University Press, 1997), 48. This discussion is based on Young, 46–53.

90. Young, *Intersecting Voices*, 46.

91. Young, *Intersecting Voices*, 48. Note how these debates about recognition have parallels to the epistemological debates about standpoint and perspective discussed earlier.

92. Young, *Intersecting Voices*, 48. Minow cites the following example: "A police captain admitted his role in the shooting of thirteen people, and asked the victims' families for forgiveness. Instead, he was met by what a *New York Times* reporter describes as "low grumbling," clarified later as a clear resistance to the notion that amnesty and truth could heal wounds." The structure of the Truth and Reconciliation Commission (TRC) in South Africa could

not stop those seeking amnesty to publicly confess merely in order to keep their jobs in the police force. Minow defends the work of the TRC but acknowledges its imperfections. She writes, "Other alleged perpetrators lie to the commission, distort their actions, respond with arrogance and adversariness, or admit their crimes in monotones, with no embarrassment." Minow, *Between Vengeance and Forgiveness* (Boston: Beacon Press, 1998), 77.

93. See María Pía Lara's discussion in *Moral Textures* (Cambridge: Polity Press, 1998), 152. Herman argues for the importance of the public discourse on trauma as well.

94. Willet, 87, 171.

95. Kelly Oliver, *Witnessing: Beyond Recognition* (Minneapolis: University of Minnesota Press, 2001), 11.

96. Oliver, *Witnessing*, 9.

97. See my discussion of the role of ambivalence and negativity in Irigaray's ethics in "Irigaray, Evil, and Negativity," in *Reading The Ethics of Sexual Difference*, ed. Debra Bergoffen and Hugh Silverman (Evanston: Northwestern University Press, forthcoming 2003). I would argue that although Irigaray does not sufficiently develop her analysis of ambivalence in both intimate and nonintimate relations, she does open up avenues for this inquiry that are bypassed by Oliver.

98. Oliver, *Witnessing*, 105.

99. Ziarek, *Dissensus*, 1.

100. Ziarek, *Dissensus*, 49–50.

101. Ziarek, *Dissensus*, 74–75.

102. Ziarek, *Dissensus*, 214.

103. Ziarek, *Dissensus*, 200, 94.

104. Ziarek, *Dissensus*, 184.

105. Susan Neiman, *Evil in Modern Thought: An Alternative History of Philosophy* (Princeton, N.J.: Princeton University Press), 272–73.

CHAPTER FOUR

~

Transnational Feminism

In this book I have tried to show that feminist philosophy is central to an interpretation of philosophy's past, by engaging with and reinterpreting the history of philosophy. I have also tried to show that feminist philosophy is vital for philosophy's tasks of reflecting on the present, in relation to the theory and practices of knowledge, and the violent conflicts that demand to be addressed by contemporary ethics. In the last chapter I discussed my own research to illustrate one way in which feminist ethical reflection takes place and how this work contributes to analyses of oppression and to theories of subjectivity and recognition. By way of conclusion, I will briefly indicate why I think that feminist philosophy is also central to the future of philosophy.

But first of all, does feminist philosophy have a future? Since the start of the new millennium, several feminist journals have posed the question of the future. One Dutch feminist journal asked readers, Would feminist philosophy exist at the end of the twenty-first century? All but one of the respondents answered yes. The single philosopher who answered no argued that by the end of this century the structural differences between men and women and the naturalizing character of gender categories would be removed, so that it would no longer be necessary to have a specifically *feminist* intervention.

Although such an optimistic assessment is appealing, the current situation of women worldwide points as much to obstacles to progress as it does to positive developments. Feminist philosophy analyzes the relation between knowledge and power—both the positive relation by which knowledge enables empowerment and the negative relation by which certain forms of knowledge are legitimized on the basis of social domination and exclusion.[1] As long as there exist forms of power that are tied to men and women's personal, institutional, and symbolic relations, feminist philosophy will have vital importance. Moreover, sexual difference will be an ongoing site for critical and creative philosophical reflection. Hence, even while feminist philosophy contributes to many of the systematic tasks of philosophy related to questions of existence, temporality, and science, it is also a practical philosophy. Like other forms of practical philosophy, it sometimes provides guidelines for specific moral and political questions. But more basically, feminist philosophy is a philosophy of protest and resistance against the ways in which power negatively shapes human lives and thoughts and an attempt to generate viable alternatives.

Because of the practical nature of feminist philosophy, its future is tied to the future of feminism. So one essential component of the question, Does feminist philosophy have a future? is the question, Does feminism have a future? In Scandinavia, many young women have begun to come out as feminists, after years of a public perception of feminists of the 1960s and 1970s as male-bashing bra-burners without sex appeal. The daughters of "red stockings," as Danish feminists of the late 1960s were dubbed, have rebelled against their mothers by wearing lipstick, nail polish, and spike heels. But many of them now are also angry.[2] Young feminists are angry about the marketing of G-string underpants to seven-year-old girls,[3] the proliferation of bare breasts in public, the cultural restrictions that make teenage girls feel that they should not be *too* good in school, the way boys' world views are given legitimacy whereas girls' world views are not, the ways boys' confidence is built up at the price of girls' loss of integrity. In short, they are angry about what Swedish women frankly call the subordination of women. Danish women are more hesitant to use this phrase and instead criticize the contemporary construction of gender for both men and women. But young feminists in Sweden, Denmark, and Norway are angry that the national and international perceptions of gender equality in the Scandinavian welfare states do not correspond to reality.

A recent report on gender and power in Denmark has confirmed that gender relations are still very much skewed in favor of men.[4] Although the majority of university students are women, only 19 percent of assistant and associate professors are women and only 8 percent of professors are women. These figures compare negatively with both Finland, where 20 percent of professors are women, and Sweden, which has 13 percent but a goal of expanding to 25 percent by 2008. Countries like Greece and Portugal are far in advance of Denmark in terms of percentage of women employed at universities.[5] University leaders in Denmark typically argue that gender equality will be achieved naturally, requiring no special initiatives. Yet the feminist statistician Inge Henningsen has argued that, based on the current rate at which universities hire women, it will take 248 years to achieve gender equality. In the public sector in Denmark, men hold 85–90 percent of the top posts. Just as in 1953, only one in twenty department heads is a woman. The gender gap in wages is currently 10–12 percent.[6] And the gendered division of labor at home has led one Swedish researcher to observe that a lucky man finds a woman to take care of everything, and a lucky woman finds a man to take care of half. The European Union's goal of *mainstreaming*, or integrating, gender issues into public policy and development, is well in advance of Danish policy and could be used as a positive ally for feminists who seek to make equality a collective issue.[7]

Not only are employment and pay equity contemporary issues in Scandinavia but also, tragically, so is violence against women. Inger Lovkrona, professor of ethnography at Lund University in Sweden, reports that one in four women in Sweden has been a victim of violence or threats of violence by a man. Although a national day of mourning was observed when Fadime Sahindal was buried after being shot and killed by her father in a so-called honor killing, there was no such public display of mourning during the course of 2001 when sixteen Swedish women were killed by their husbands.[8] Public attention is given to violence committed by immigrant men, which is attributed to their specific culture, though culture is not blamed when natives of

Scandinavian countries commit violence. Instead, journalists and experts focus on how social and psychological stress contribute to individual men's violent behavior.

Men commit terrible acts of violence against women in many parts of the world. In Bangladesh, there is a horrifying new trend in which attackers throw acid on their victims, whose skin melts away along with their semblance of human form—a source of lifelong pain and grotesque mutilation. In 2001 there were 338 attacks. Two-thirds of the victims were women, and one-third of them were under eighteen years of age. Men attacked women because they felt that they had received too little in dowry or because they had been rejected by a woman and wanted to destroy her chances of getting another suitor. The victims of the attacks are viewed as polluted and often rejected by their families.[9]

In another horrifying instance of violence against women, a village jury in Pakistan on 22 June 2002, ordered that a twenty-eight-year-old woman named Mukhtaran Bibi be gang raped. Her twelve-year-old brother had been abducted by three men, sodomized, held hostage in a room with a woman in her late twenties, and later accused of having an affair with the woman. A government investigation subsequently verified that the boy was too young to "meet the sexual lust of any opposite sex."[10] Although Ms. Bibi was chosen by her family to publicly apologize for the brother, when she appeared before the tribal council, the *panchayat*, it ordered four men to rape her. After the rapes, which lasted one and a half hours, the men "danced in jubilation" and Ms. Bibi was forced to walk home naked before three hundred people. Just six days later, Naseem Mai, a twenty-six-year-old woman in the next village, was raped by one man while two other men held her at gunpoint. She killed herself two days later when she saw the guilty man escape police arrest.[11] During the first half of 2002, seventy-two gang rapes and ninety-three other rapes were documented in Punjab Province alone, although it is estimated that a woman is raped every six hours and a woman is gang raped every four days. Since the rape of Ms. Bibi, which gained national and international attention, reported rapes have increased. Some police chiefs dismiss these reports as fabricated. But because a rape conviction requires two witnesses, and since 60 percent of women who lodge a complaint are themselves later charged with having extramarital sex, fabricated reports are highly unlikely.

On 19 August 2002, in Funtua, Nigeria, an Islamic court condemned thirty-one-year-old Amina Lawal to death by stoning for having had sexual relations outside marriage. Ms. Lawal admitted to having sexual intercourse with a man who had promised to marry her. The man had previously admitted paternity to Ms. Lawal's child, and had paid for the festivities following the child's birth, but denied that he was the child's father in front of the Islamic court. Ms. Lawal's execution was ordered to take place in a couple of years, after the child is weaned. Her lawyers will appeal the decision in two higher courts.[12]

In addition to these recent atrocities, 100–130 million women and girls worldwide have had female genital mutilation (FGM) performed on them. This practice usually involves removal of the clitoris and often the removal of the inner and outer labia. In its most extreme form, infibulation, almost all of the external genitalia are cut away, the flesh from the outer labia is sewn together, and a small hole is left for urination and menstruation. It can result in death and lifelong physical and psychological debilities.[13] Almost half the women in Africa have been circumcised, and this practice is being brought to the United States and Europe through immigration. France, Canada, Denmark, Switzerland, Sweden, and Belgium have all outlawed the practice.

Selling women into prostitution across national borders, described as the slave trade of women, is another feature of the contemporary global order. For example, prostitution is now booming in Kosovo, with numerous strip clubs where men buy sex with dancers. Clubs are staffed with foreign women from Romania, Moldova, and the Ukraine. The International Organization of Migration reports that 70 percent of foreign women were lured from their home countries by promises of work as cleaners, waitresses, baby-sitters, or care workers. But local women are not safe from this slave trade either, and one Kosovar girl who sought sanctuary at a safe house run by the Centre for the Protection of Women and Children reported having been kept a virtual slave in a nightclub in Mitrovica for two years. Her clientele consisted of local men and international military personnel.[14]

Feminists will continue to protest and resist these economic, political, cultural, psychological, and physical affronts. However, there are critics who argue that the term "feminism" is complicitous in the very power structures that it protests, and that it is a Western notion with little relevance to women in Islamic countries. In Egypt, despite the fact that in 1999 only two women were elected to parliament (though other women were appointed to parliament), there is dispute among women as to whether a feminist movement is the correct strategy.[15] The debate about how to relate the struggle for women's dignity and rights with Islam is not new. In 1923, Huda Sha'rawi formed the Egyptian Feminist Association to fight for women's rights within the bounds of Islam. Huda Sha'rawi argued that men and women should share power. The difficulty in this task lay not with Islam, but in the way in which Islam was practiced. However, some people viewed her position as too radical. Zaynab al-Ghazali began a woman's movement that was decidedly more Muslim in character and is today a mentor for women Islamicists in Egypt. The doctor and author Nawal al-Sa'adawi is more explicitly antireligious. But her position is so controversial in Egypt that she has moved the headquarters for her Arab Women's Solidarity Organization to Washington. Many of the women who are active in Islamic movements hold themselves aloof from feminism. But they follow Huda Sha'rawi's lead in focusing on the opposition between the values of dignity attributed to women in the Koran and the reality of women's position in Muslim countries.[16] Women who are active in Islamic movements emphasize that personal development requires social engagement; consequently, the movement has had the effect of mobilizing women to participate in political praxis.[17] These examples indicate that women's struggle for dignity, education, and access to political participation may use very different strategies than those that characterize Western feminism.

Thus, not all movements to mobilize women for social engagement consider themselves to be feminist. Moreover, many women are critical of the presuppositions and methodologies of Western feminists, who often use the concept of "third world woman" as a condensed symbol of oppression, subordination, and victimhood. The feminist scholar and activist Chandra Talpade Mohanty argues that many Western feminists, as well as middle-class urban scholars from Africa or Asia, implicitly assume the West as their primary referent for theory and praxis.

These scholars codify non-Western women as Other, as ignorant, tradition-bound victims lacking in autonomy, while Western women are portrayed as educated, modern, with the freedom to make decisions about their bodies and their lives. This ethnocentric universalism can be viewed as a form of intellectual colonization of non-Western women. As such, it is blind to the particular geographic, historical, and cultural complexity that must ground feminist strategies.[18]

Hence, there is a contestation among scholars and activists over the language of protest and resistance. Already in the mid-1980s, the Indian-born scholar Gayatri Spivak argued that attempts to make Western feminism more inclusive by including the figure of the "third world woman" are deeply flawed, since this figure is itself crucial to the subject formation of privileged women of the first world.[19] Thus, the language of "global feminism" has also become suspect. This phrase presumes the radical feminist emphasis that gender is the primary basis of oppression and seems to suggest that there is or ought to be a women's movement that spans the whole world. Instead, many commentators are beginning to refer to "feminism in a global frame" in order to emphasize the localized contexts in which movements of women's resistance exist.[20]

The phrase "international feminism" is also highly problematic, in that it often refers to an ideological package put together by well-financed, neo-liberal interests in the United States.[21] For example, when the U.S. women's soccer team won the Women's World Cup by defeating the team from the People's Republic of China in July 1999, U.S. press coverage focused exclusively on the triumph of a particularly American way of empowering women. These assumptions are often present in many United Nations or Ford Foundation–sponsored projects for furthering women's human rights and global democratization. Thus, international feminism has been criticized for presuming that the United States provides the model of justice and empowerment that should be exported to women in all other countries—a move that makes the achievements of women in other countries disappear. The belief that an American way of feminism is best expresses a desire for epistemological authority over other women that precludes engaging in the history of thought in non-Western countries. Hence, this approach can hardly be called international.

To highlight the need for a different practice, some theorists have introduced the phrase "transnational feminism." This phrase keeps the tension between the root *national*—the fact that an individual's political rights depend on citizenship in specific nation-states—and the prefix *trans*—the fact that both economic corporations and public spheres cross national boundaries.[22] Transnational collaboration of feminists can be based on the notion of similarity—e.g., as with communities in the Philippines, South Korea, and Japan that all have had experience with the stationing of foreign military facilities. Or transnational collaboration can be based on a notion of mutual implication in structures of inequality, whereby the privileges of some women are linked in a structured way to the lack of privileges of other women—e.g., through chains of production and consumption. But transnational collaboration depends on giving up the essentializing views of culture evident in what Indian-born philosopher Uma Narayan calls the Package Picture. The Package Picture ignores the specific historical and political processes through which certain values and practices are taken to be central components of a culture. For example, dominant members of a culture often are willing to discard certain practices but resist other cultural changes. Frequently, the changes they resist are those pertaining to the welfare of women, as in the insistence on preserving female circumcision (i.e., FGM) rites. In some cases, new laws (for example, laws that eliminate the distinction between adultery and rape in Pakistan) are instituted under the auspices of preserving tradition, e.g., "Muslim law," even when such laws are counter to tradition.[23] Only when one gives up a homogenizing view of culture and sees how domination operates in processes of cultural preservation and transformation is it possible to see affinities of values between, e.g., Western feminists and Indian or Pakistani feminists.[24]

Given that feminist praxis and theory must be referenced to these complex cultural and transnational relations, what tasks does feminist philosophy face in the future? Of course, attempting to predict future developments is the surest way to lose friends, as amateur stockbrokers no doubt can attest. For philosophy, as for history, the closest one can come to future projections is an analysis of how the tensions and contradictions of the present might develop or be overcome. For feminists living in Europe, one of the central tasks is to deal with the implications of the European Union. The project of European unification, originating in post–World War II as an economic agreement to control raw materials and a strategy to prevent future wars, contains both conservative and progressive possibilities. As Rosi Braidotti writes, conservative forces seek to set the agenda for creating a "Fortress Europe" syndrome that would install an ethnically "pure" and self-sufficient Europe. A progressive European project, on the other hand, would give priority to constructing a European identity based on resistance to war, nationalism, xenophobia, racism, and sexism.[25] The theoretical implications of this struggle are to put the analyses of militarization, nationalism, xenophobia, and racism in the forefront in work in feminist philosophy.

Feminist philosophers have begun to argue for specific interventions against mechanisms that maintain neo-liberal globalization. Alison Jaggar describes this neo-liberal order, which supports "free trade" so that business owners can move production to areas of the world where wages are lowest, though it controls the movement of workers seeking higher wages. The ideology of neo-liberalism opposes government regulation of wages, working conditions, and environmental protections. Neo liberals urge governments to abandon social welfare responsibilities and to bring all economically exploitable resources into private ownership. Jaggar argues that engaging in a critical evaluation of global neo-liberalism and developing alternatives is not only one of the most urgent tasks facing moral and political philosophy but one of the most urgent tasks for feminist philosophy because of the harm caused by neo-liberal globalization to most of the world's women. Jaggar exemplifies this project by arguing that Northern Hemisphere countries have a moral obligation to "forgive" the debt of Southern Hemisphere countries. She argues that (1) much of the south's dependence on the north is a fictitious construct of a systematically biased global accounting system; (2) the dependence of the north on the south for resources, labor, and markets exceeds the dependence of the south on the north; and (3) the dependence of the south was produced by a history of violent exploitation. Hence, aid payments from the north should be viewed as reparations, not charity, and the term debt "forgiveness" is misleading. More appropriately, it is the north that should be seeking moral, if not economic forgiveness, from the south.[26]

Transnational issues should also inform feminist work in the history of philosophy. Since the project of international feminism has claimed epistemological authority for Western European and American culture, it has precluded an engagement with the history of thought of other cultures. To challenge the presumption of epistemological authority for Western countries, feminists need to join in cross-cultural philosophical work that breaks with the myth that being a native of a specific geographical location gives one special access or insight into German idealism, French existentialism, American pragmatism, or Indian Vedanta.[27] This myth has contributed to essentialist thinking that underlines xenophobia, as in the French anti-Semites' contention that only *real* Frenchmen who possess the secret of soil and country—and not Jews—could understand French poetry.[28] Since, in the West, philosophy becomes identical with the work produced by philosophers at universities, it is also crucial to challenge the insistence on maintaining education exclusively in the Western canon. This policy prevents students from learning the philosophical traditions of other cultures and is responsible for reinforcing the myth of a mysterious, mythical, nonrational East.

Transnational perspectives have implications for feminist work in epistemology as well. Feminist philosophers are pursuing projects about how the scope and use of knowledge intersects with gender issues and the status of women in particular cultures, as well as studying the implications of differences between speculative and oral traditions.[29] This work not only protests against the discrimination of women as knowers in given cultures but also explores how women can reappropriate knowledge categories and contribute to more egalitarian epistemologies.

Numerous other issues that are already under debate will continue to demand future attention: issues of equality and affirmative action; the new reproductive technologies and the technologies of destruction; pornography and prostitution; theories of sexuality and the relation between queer and feminist theory; theories of democracy and analyses of the "other"; theories of autonomy and of the relational self; metaphysical analysis of materiality and temporality. The list extends far beyond the material I have discussed in this book.

My goal has neither been to present the entirety of the scope of feminist philosophy to the reader, nor to present it as a field that has finished making its primary conceptual contributions. Rather, I have selected a few key areas within feminist philosophy to show the significance of its contributions over the past fifty years. Feminist philosophy is a developing field whose path is not entirely foreseeable. The field of feminist philosophy is not only open in terms of its future development but also in terms of its relation to traditional fields in philosophy. Feminist philosophers have engaged in serious dialogue in the history of philosophy, epistemology, and ethics, as well as in other fields not discussed here, such as aesthetics, philosophy of language, and political philosophy. It is now time for these fields to be open to feminism. Only if mainstream philosophy incorporates a knowledge of and dialogue with feminist philosophy can it hope to change the structure of the reproduction of knowledge in the academy—a sorely needed social and intellectual change in Denmark. But feminist philosophy is not concerned with the interconnections between knowledge and power alone, though these are central issues. Feminist philosophy is fundamentally a contribution to philosophy. It carries out one of the oldest tasks of philosophy—to serve as a gadfly. Feminist philosophers poke at many of the sore points that philosophers have preferred to ignore, sore points that reveal fundamental insights into men's and women's position in and understanding of the world. As such, it makes a vital contribution to both the present and future of philosophy.

Notes

1. Jane Duran, *Worlds of Knowing: Global Feminist Epistemologies* (New York: Routledge, 2001), 145.

2. Sarah Cawood discussed the Scandinavian publications by young feminists at the Gender Research conference in Aarhus, Denmark, 20 April 2002; Linda Norrman Skugge and Belinda Olsson, eds., *Fittstim* (Stockholm: DN

forlag, 1999); Hilde Charlotte Solheim and Helle Vaagland, eds., *Raatekst* (Oslo: H. Aschehoug and Co., 1999); Anita Frank Goth, ed., *Nu er det nok* (Copenhagen: Rosinante, 2000); and Leonora Christina Skov, ed., *De røde sko: Feminisme nu* (Copenhagen: Tiderne Skifter, 2002). Cawood argued that the Swedish strategy, with its emphasis on subordination and subversion, is the most effective strategy for social change. The Danish strategy, with its emphasis on gender constructivism as an expression of an individualistic–liberal culture, is least likely to contribute to a social movement for change.

3. A few days after the Danish supermarket chain Kvickly starting selling G-string underpants in children's sizes, fifteen-year-old Cecil Skovløber wrote a letter of protest to Ekstra Bladet, which began a public debate. The head of information for Coop Denmark, Jens Juul Jensen, defended the marketing strategy by claiming, "Vi gør ikke noget etisk forkert. Der er ikke noget seksuelt over en g-streng. Det er blot endnu et område, hvor børnene forsøger at ligne de voksne." (Translation: "We are not doing anything unethical. There is nothing sexual about a G-string. It is just another area where children try to be like adults.") After massive protest from customers, the chain withdrew the G-string underpants the following day. Jens Juul Jensen said, "Der er åbenbart mere sex i en g-streng end vi havde regnet med." (Translation: "Apparently there is more sex in a G-string than we thought.") Trine Maria Ilsøe, "Kvickly alene med sex undertøj til småbørn," *Politiken*, 1 August 2002, 4 and "Kvickly dropper g-streng til børn," Trine Maria Ilsøe, *Politiken*, 2 August 2002, 1.

4. Anette Borchorst, ed., *Kønsmagt under forandring* (Copenhagen: Hans Reitzel, 2002). Unless otherwise noted, the statistics in this paragraph are drawn from the article "Køn og eliter" by Peter Munk Christiansen, Birgit Møller, and Lise Togeby, 72–87.

5. *Lige Til*, nr. 2 (December 2001): 7. This is a publication of the *Videnscenter for Ligestilling*, whose public funding has been totally eliminated by the current government in Denmark.

6. Karen Sjørup and Anette Dina Sørensen, "Kvinderne tager magten–myten længe leve," *Politiken*, 2 August 2002, section 2, 4.

7. Annette Bjørg Koeller, "Ligestilling som skuvaerdi," *Forum*, www.forum.kvinfo.dk/forum.asp?Page ID=49922, 7 [accessed 8 March 2002].

8. Interview with Inger Lovkrona by Anne-Mette Klausen, "Men slår da kvinder," in *Forum*, www.forum.kvinfo.dk/forum.asp?PageID49939 [accessed 15 May 2002].

9. Ulrik Jantzen, "Ætsede for altid," *Berlingske Tidende*, 12 May 2002, section 2, 6.

10. Ian Fisher, "Account of Punjab Rape Tells of a Brutal Society," *New York Times*, 17 July 2002, A3.

11. Ian Fisher, "Seeing No Justice, a Rape Victim Chooses Death," *New York Times*, 28 July 2002. The family of the rapist was said to have bribed a police officer—the same officer who was accused of misconduct in the case of Mukhtaran Bibi.

12. Jesper Strudsholm, "Hun skal stenes, når amningen stopper" and "Steningssag truer med at splitte Nigeria," *Politiken*, 20 August 2002.

13. Linda Burstyn, "Female Circumcision Comes to America," *The Atlantic Online*, www.theatlantic.com/unbound/flashhbks/fgm/fgm.htm, October 1995, 5 [accessed 15 May 2002]. See also Alice Walker, *Possessing the Secret of Joy*. Rachel Horner, in the *Concord Times*, reported the death of a fourteen-year-old girl after having undergone circumcision in Freetown, the capital of Sierra Leone (allafrica.com/stories/200207310264.html [accessed 2 May 2003]). The philosopher Diana Tietjens Meyers has discussed the concept of personal autonomy in relation to female genital cutting. See "Feminism and Women's Autonomy. The Challenge of Female Genital Cutting," in *Metaphilosophy* (October 2000); also in *The Edinburgh Companion to Contemporary Liberalism*, ed. Mark Evans (Edinburgh: Edinburgh University Press, forthcoming).

14. Jeta Xharra, "Kosovo Sex Industry," www.iwpr.net [accessed 6 August 2002].

15. In 1982, Egypt instituted the Jihan-law, which would assure that at least 10 percent of the members of parliament should be women. If they are not elected, then women are appointed. Jordan has begun discussing whether to introduce a quota system to ensure that at least 20–30 percent of parliament is made up of women. Connie Carøe Christiansen, "Islamisk aktivisme skal forbedre skæve kønsforhold," *Forum*, www.forum.kvinfo.dk/forum.asp? Page ID=39887, 27 August 1999, 3 [accessed 23 May 2002].

16. Christiansen, "Islamsk aktivisme," 5.

17. Christiansen, "Muslimske kvinder i action," manuscript, 1.

18. Chandra Talpade Mohanty, "Under Western Eyes: Feminist Scholarship and Colonial Discourses," in Chandra Talpade Mohanty, Ann Russo, and Lourdes Torres, eds., *Third World Women and the Politics of Feminism* (Bloomington: Indiana University Press, 1991), 51–80.

19. Gayatri Spivak, "Three Women's Texts and a Critique of Imperialism," in *"Race," Writing and Difference*, ed. Henry Louis Gates Jr. (Chicago: University of Chicago Press, 1985), 262–80.

20. Vera Mackie, "The Language of Globalization, Transnationality and Feminism," in *International Feminist Journal of Politics* 3, no. 2 (August 2001): 182.

21. Tani Barlow, "International Feminism of the Future," in *Signs: Journal of Women in Culture and Society* 25, no. 4 (Summer 2000): 1098–105.

22. Mackie, "The Language of Globalization," 180–206. Mackie cites Nancy Fraser's phrase "transnational feminist counter-public" to refer to feminist communications across national borders, 189. See Nancy Fraser, *Justice Interruptus: Critical Reflections on the "Postsocialist" Condition* (London: Routledge, 1997).

23. For example, in Pakistan General Zia ul-Haq introduced a law in 1979 requiring the presence of four witnesses to an act of adultery or rape before a crime can be established. This law obliterates the distinction between them and makes rape a private matter with the burden of proof belonging to the victim. Been Sarwar, "Pakistan: Brutality Cloaked as Tradition,"www.wlum.org/english/new-archives/pakistan/brutal-cloaked-as-tradition-august-2002.htm [accessed 2 May 2003].

24. Uma Narayan, "Undoing the 'Package Picture' of Cultures," in *Signs: Journal of Women in Culture and Society* 5, no. 4 (Summer 2000): 1083–86. Narayan refers to Olayinka Koso-Thomas's book *The Circumcision of Women* (New York: Zed, 1987). In Sierra Leone, elaborate initiation rites that were preliminaries to female circumcision have been given up for lack of time, money, and social infrastructure. But the rite of excision remains, since dominant members claim it is crucial for "preserving tradition." See note 12.

25. Rosi Braidotti, "Once Upon a Time in Europe," in *Signs: Journal of Women in Culture and Society* 25, no. 4 (Summer 2000): 1061–64.

26. Alison Jaggar, "A Feminist Critique of the Alleged Southern Debt," *Wissen/Macht/Geschlecht*, ed. Angelica Baum et al. (Zurich: Chronos, 2002), 11–40. Jaggar notes that citizens are held economically responsible for debts undertaken by their governments, often even before they were born. She calculates that every baby born in the developing world today owes 482 dollars at birth.

27. Anindita N. Balslev, "Cross-Cultural Conversation: Its Scope and Aspirations," in *Cross-Cultural Conversation*, ed. Anindita Niyogi Balslev (Atlanta: Scholars Press, 1966), 15–27. Anindita Balslev has fought so far without success to influence departments of philosophy in Denmark to introduce courses in Indian philosophy. Needless to say, there are no offerings in African or Chinese philosophy either.

28. Jean-Paul Sartre, *Anti-Semite and Jew*, trans. George J. Becker (New York: Schocken Books, 1948), 24.

29. Duran, 4.

Index

About the Author

Robin May Schott is associate research professor and director for the NOS-H project "Sexuality, Death and the Feminine: Feminist Philosophical Analysis" at the University of Copenhagen in Denmark. In 2003–2004, she is a fellow at the Danish Institute for Advanced Studies in the Humanities. *Discovering Feminist Philosophy* is her fourth book.